D1559404

diseases of marine
aquarium fishes

Mark P. Dulin, D.V.M., M.S.

FRONTISPIECE:
Miss Karen Mason dissecting a parrotfish. Photo by Dr. Herbert R. Axelrod.

Distributed in the U.S.A. by T.F.H. Publications, Inc., 211 West Sylvania Avenue, P.O. Box 27, Neptune City, N.J. 07753; in England by T.F.H. (Gt. Britain) Ltd., 13 Nutley Lane, Reigate, Surrey; in Canada to the book store and library trade by Clarke, Irwin & Company, Clarwin House, 791 St. Clair Avenue West, Toronto 10, Ontario; in Canada to the pet trade by Rolf C. Hagen Ltd., 3225 Sartelon Street, Montreal 382, Quebec; in Southeast Asia by Y.W. Ong, 9 Lorong 36 Geylang, Singapore 14; in Australia and the south Pacific by Pet Imports Pty. Ltd., P.O. Box 149, Brookvale 2100, N.S.W., Australia. Published by T.F.H. Publications, Inc. Ltd., The British Crown Colony of Hong Kong.

Contents

Acknowledgments

My special thanks to Dr. George (Bill) W. Klontz for providing me with a veterinarian's approach to the science of fish health and for his constant encouragement during my graduate studies.

I wish to express my most sincere appreciation to Dr. Stanislas F. Snieszko for reviewing my manuscript and for providing much insight into the diagnosis and treatment of fish diseases. I also want to thank Mr. Murray Wiener for his advice and assistance with the drug toxicity tests and Mr. Tom Alcorn for his line drawings.

To Brian Jonathan Dulin
whose fascination with nature's simple beauty
. . . makes me happy

ABBREVIATED DIAGNOSIS AND TREATMENT CHART

Refer to the page numbers opposite the condensed list of clinical signs for detailed diagnosis and treatment procedures.

	Clinical Signs and Pathological Changes:	Diagnosis:	Treatment:
100	All fishes affected. Distress, jumping, erratic swimming, rapid breathing, opercles flared, gills exposed.	NONSPECIFIC; COULD BE HYPOXIA, TOO HIGH TEMPERATURE, OR POISONING.	Change water immediately. Increase aeration. Check water chemistries.
101	Most of fishes affected. Dead fishes have mouth agape, opercles flared, pale gills; rigor mortis sets in fast.	ANOXIA.	Increase dissolved oxygen. Reduce number of tank inhabitants.
102	Most of fishes affected. Listless, rapid breathing, pin-point hemorrhages on thymus, chocolate brown blood.	NITRITE TOXICITY.	Put fish in treatment tank. Add 1 ppm methylene blue and 250 mg vitamin C per 10 gal. water. Evaluate cause of ammonia nitrogen build up and correct.
103	Few to several fishes affected. External parasites visible, rapid breathing; fishes scratch opercula.	ECTOPARASITISM CAUSED BY MONOGENETIC FLUKES.	Remove with tweezers or 3 min. freshwater bath, or up to a 30 min. formalin bath.
105	Few to many fishes affected. Copepods, or the egg sacs of copepods, are seen attached to the gills or the skin of the fishes.	COPEPOD PARASITISM.	Put all fish in treatment tank. 1 ppm Dylox for up to four treatments.
107	One to several fishes affected. White-gray, cotton wool-like lesions on skin.	FUNGUS (SAPROLEGNIA) INFECTION.	Swab affected area with either hydrogen peroxide, Mercurochrome, iodine tincture solution, or malachite green solution. Put fish in treatment tank for Furanace treatment.

#	Symptoms	Disease	Treatment
	Several to many fishes affected. Difficult respiration, "flashing," small powdery spots on skin and fins. White areas on gills.	WHITE SPOT DISEASE.	Remove invertebrates from exhibition tank, give them a freshwater bath then keep them in the quarantine tank for the next 2 weeks. Treat fish in exhibition tank for 2 weeks with 0.15 ppm free copper ions.
111	Usually solitary fish affected. Listless, jerking, twitching, whirling dizzily.	ICHTHYOPHONUS INFECTION, A SYSTEMIC FUNGUS INFECTION.	Remove fish from exhibition tank. No proven cure.
112	One to several fishes affected. Exophthalmos, ascites, roughened scales, necrosis and abscesses on kidney, liver, and spleen.	KIDNEY DISEASE.	Put affected fish in treatment tank. Erythromycin 250 mg/5 gal. of water for 5 to 7 days.
114	Usually only one fish affected. Exophthalmos, frayed fins, blotchy skin, ulcerated areas, nodules in body organs.	TUBERCULOSIS.	Isoniazid 250 mg/5 gal. water. Rifampin in food.
117	Most of fishes affected. Clouded eyes, frayed fins. Reddening at base of fins, vent, along lateral line, and mouth. Reddening of internal body tissues, enlarged liver and spleen.	ACUTE SYSTEMIC BACTERIAL INFECTION.	Put affected fish into treatment tank. Treat with broad spectrum antibiotic such as Chloromycetin, gentamycin, kanamycin, or neomycin for 5 to 7 days.
121	Most fishes develop bubbles beneath the skin and within the fins. Exophthalmos.	GAS-BUBBLE DISEASE.	Not a problem in warm water aquariums. Rid tank of excess gas. Repair pump.
123	One to several fishes begin wasting away. Worms in intestines.	INTESTINAL ROUNDWORM OR TAPEWORMS.	Piperazine for roundworms. Yomesan® for tapeworms.
123	One to several fishes develop wart-like lesions on the body, especially around the fins and mouth.	LYMPHOCYSTIS.	Quarantine affected fish for at least 2 months. Self cure. Severe cases may require liquid nitrogen therapy or surgical removal.

The author reflects upon the health of a triggerfish and an angelfish. This type of visual examination is a daily necessity. Photo by Dr. Herbert R. Axelrod.

A butterflyfish, *Chaetodon collare,* in perfect health. Photo by Klaus Paysan.

Introduction

With increasing urbanization it is becoming increasingly impractical for many people to keep a cat or dog as a family pet. Each year many people are switching to keeping birds and fishes for pets, as evidenced by increased sales of these animals and their accompanying cages, tanks, food, and equipment. Annual U.S. sales of fishes, aquariums, tank accessory items, and fish food have risen to the billion dollar mark, thus reflecting an ever-expanding number of tropical fish hobbyists (aquarists).

Aquarists are becoming more sophisticated in their field and are beginning to demand quality and variety in their fishes and related aquarium products. Keeping exotic marine fishes in captivity is becoming more and more popular, and the success rate of maintaining these fishes is increasing as well. Much of this success can be attributed to a heightened awareness on the part of saltwater aquarists. Several excellent reference books are available on setting up and maintaining the marine aquarium, and these books undoubtedly are partially responsible for this heightened awareness.

Advances have been made in the art of providing saltwater species with suitable habitats for growth. Setting up and maintaining a marine aquarium can be considered an art, but the fishes are not mere decorative possessions for your home or office. Whenever you assume ownership of an animal you must also assume responsibility for its health and well being. Sophisticated aquarium set-ups, along with water quality monitoring and treatment kits, have provided many aquarists with an armamentarium not available to many other pet species.

Even with this sophisticated equipment and reference material, many aquarists seem doomed to dismal failure in the art of raising exotic marine species in captivity. This is not always the fault of the hobbyist; even conscientious aquarists have disease problems in their carefully maintained fish tanks.

Aquatic animal medicine is still in its infancy, resembling the backward state of the poultry industry some 30 years ago. Fisheries scientists had previously devoted most of their efforts to the isolation and classification of fish pathogens, and only relatively recently have they turned to the prevention, diagnosis, and cure of fish diseases. Veterinarians have been slow to recognize the marine fish field as a specialty area, so community expertise on fish health problems is generally lacking. Hopefully the next decade will bring about changes in this regard, but until fish disease diagnostics and treatments become available on the local level, aquarists will be left to fend for themselves. Certainly experts *are* in existence throughout the United States; generally, however, they are too busy with teaching, research, or caring for their own marine fishes. Even if one could find a qualified fish disease expert to examine affected fishes it could very well be too late by the time a diagnosis was made. Generally, once the clinical signs of disease have developed in captive marine tropical fishes, treatment must be initiated promptly or death may rapidly ensue.

Currently, several universities and private firms are actively conducting research on new drugs to be used for the control and treatment of fish diseases. Immunizing agents for various fish diseases show much promise and will likely be available during the next decade. Fishes are currently being immunized by injection, by the oral route, and more recently by immersion into a solution of the bacterial antigen. When these fish vaccines are perfected, aquarists will be able to purchase marine fishes which have been previously immunized against many of the common fish pathogens in much the same way as a dog is immunized against distemper and hepatitis.

Until such time that local diagnostic and treatment services, along with new pharmaceutical agents, become available, however, you as a marine fish hobbyist will continue to have to rely largely on your own management and medical techniques.

The purpose of this book is to provide you with a simple yet straightforward guide to maintaining health in the marine aquarium. I have purposely tried to stay away from complicated or impractical diagnostic methodology. Noninfectious diseases such as nitrite toxicity, low dissolved oxygen, and malnutrition must be adequately diagnosed before successful treatment can be accomplished. Infectious diseases, however, need not always be diagnosed to the particular organism causing the disease in order to initiate a successful treatment. It is likewise not always necessary and practical to grow the causative pathogen on artificial media and conduct antibacterial sensitivity tests before treatment is begun. Realistically, this bacteriological approach is impractical for the hobbyist, and the delay encountered during this procedure could well result in the demise of the affected fish.

Physicians rely heavily on symptoms of disease to support a tentative diagnosis. In treating human diseases, treatment is generally initiated prior to awaiting a definitive diagnosis from the laboratory. If medical doctors can initiate treatment without a definitive diagnosis based on bacteriological and histopathological techniques, then the aquarist is justified in doing likewise. Throughout this book I will encourage you to use all the diagnostic tools which are within your capabilities, but emphasis will be placed on diagnosing the disease based upon clinical signs of disease. This approach is justified because no one should be more familiar with behavioral and symptomatic changes occurring in your fishes than you yourself. By careful daily observation you can develop a close rapport with your fishes and become quick to notice any behavioral abnormalities. You will find that these daily visual inspections will be invaluable in monitoring fish health. Behavioral abnormalities generally are coincident with clinical signs of disease.

Prompt and proper action when these abnormalities occur is what separates the successful from the unsuccessful exotic marine fish aquarist. This book is intended to not only provide you with a "do-it-yourself" treatment for exotic marine fish diseases but more importantly to provide information to help *avoid* disease outbreaks.

Throughout this book I have tried to avoid the use of unnecessary technical jargon, yet at the same time provide you with some terms with which you as a marine aquarist should become familiar. Hopefully each of you will not only learn more about the art of keeping marine fishes in captivity but also increase your scientific vocabulary. The following technical terms have been used in the context of this book:

ACIDOSIS: An abnormal condition resulting from accumulation of acid or loss of base within the body tissues and fluids.

ACUTE: Having a short and relatively severe course.

ALKALOSIS: An abnormal condition resulting from accumulation of base or loss of acid within the body tissues and fluids.

ANOXIA: Absence of oxygen.

ANTIBIOTIC: A chemical substance produced by microorganisms which has the capacity to inhibit the growth of, or to destroy, bacteria and other microorganisms.

ASCITES: Accumulation of fluid within the abdominal cavity.

ASYMPTOMATIC CARRIER: An infected fish harboring a specific infectious agent in the absence of discernible clinical disease and serving as a potential source of infection to the rest of the population.

ATROPHY: A reduction in the size of a tissue or organ.

BENTHIC: Living at the bottom.

CARNIVOROUS: Subsisting or feeding on animal tissue.

CHRONIC: Persisting over a long period of time.

COPEPODS: Small crustaceans which during some stages of their development may parasitize fishes.

CORPUSCLES OF STANNIUS: Small endocrine glands situated on the peritoneal surface of the kidneys. Fishes *generally* have two of these corpuscles.

DINOFLAGELLATE: Single-celled organisms which have two flagella and are generally encased in a cellulose-like armor made up of two to many plates.

ECTOPARASITE: External parasite.

EMACIATION: A wasted condition of the body.

EPIZOOTIC: Attacking most of the fishes in the tank at the same time.

EXOPHTHALMOS: Abnormal protrusion of the eyeball.

FIBROTIC: Characterized by the formation of fibrous tissue.

GRANULOMA: A mass of inflammatory tissue usually in the form of a discrete nodule.

HERBIVOROUS: Subsisting or feeding on plant tissue.

HOST: A living animal or plant providing subsistence or lodgment to a parasite.

HYDROSTATIC PRESSURE: The pressure exerted by water at rest.

IN SITU: In the natural or normal place.

MENINGITIS: Inflammation of the membranes which envelop the brain.

MONOGENETIC TREMATODE: Trematodes that have no intermediate hosts and are usually ectoparasitic.

NECROPSY: Examination of a body after death.

NECROSIS: Death of tissue.

OMNIVOROUS: Feeding on both animal and plant tissue.

OSMOSIS: The process of diffusion across a semipermeable membrane.

PATHOGEN: An infectious agent capable of causing disease.

PATHOGNOMONIC: A distinctive or characteristic clinical sign or pathological change occurring in a disease about which a diagnosis can be made.

PELAGIC: Living in open waters, as opposed to living close to shore.

PERITONITIS: Inflammation of the membranes lining the abdomen.

pH: A measure of acidity or alkalinity expressed as the logarithm of the reciprocal of the hydrogen ion concentration.

PROTOZOAN: A single-celled animal. There are about 30,000 species of protozoans, differing greatly as to size, shape, structure, habits, reproduction, and life cycles.

RIGOR MORTIS: The stiffening of a dead body.

SAPROPHYTE: An organism capable of obtaining food by absorption of dissolved organic material, mainly by osmosis of organic break-down products.

SPORE: A unicellular resistant body, capable of development into a new individual organism.

STRESS: A physical, chemical, biological or any other environmental factor which extends the adaptive responses of the fish beyond the normal range or which disturbs the normal functioning to such an extent that the chances of survival are reduced.

SYSTEMIC: Affecting the entire body.

TREMATODE: Parasitic flatworms without segments which use a sucker-type mouth to obtain nourishment from a host.

Health-related Aspects of Setting Up a Marine Aquarium

It is beyond the scope of this book to go into much detail on setting up a saltwater aquarium. Several excellent books are available (see the "Recommended Reading" list) for those beginning aquarists who need help in establishing a suitable habitat for their marine fishes. You must keep in mind that the saltwater aquarium is a highly artificial environment and in no way should be thought of as a miniature ocean. It is only by maintaining a delicate balance of a whole complex of water chemistry parameters that fishes are able to survive in a closed system. Ideally, a single-pass, flow-through system using aerated, warmed, non-polluted salt water would be used. This continuous water flow would drastically reduce the incidence of external parasitism, toxicity from any build-up of metabolic waste byproducts, and other diseases. Of course this approach is impractical for everyone except aquariums located directly on an unpolluted coastline. In a closed system, aquarists must maintain a very delicate balance of a whole multitude of water chemistry parameters in order to keep the water quality within the fishes' range of tolerance. Controlling this environment involves a thorough understanding of marine aquarium management procedures. Some of the health-related management factors which must be considered in providing exotic marine fishes with a suitable environment, free of stress factors, are listed below.

Tank: The fish container must be free of toxic materials. It should be of adequate size to avoid overcrowding and have a cover to prevent fish from escaping.

Lighting: Most marine fishes do best with a 12-hour light/dark photoperiod. Too little light prevents normal feeding activity, while too much light may turn the water green from algal blooms.

Heating: Optimum temperature range for most tropical marine species is 76° to 78° F (25° C). Most species can survive in the range of 70° to 85° F (21° to 30° C).

There are many types of aquarium air pumps available. Deep marine aquarium tanks require a powerful pump. Photo courtesy of Penn-Plax Inc.

Aeration: A dissolved oxygen level of 7 to 8 parts per million (ppm) is desirable. This is best accomplished by using an airstone or diffuser which is adjusted to produce very tiny bubbles. Remember that increases in altitude and temperature diminish the oxygen-carrying capacity of the water. Also remember that the air pump picks up room air to oxygenate the tank. If paint fumes or tobacco smoke are in the room, these fumes can be forced into solution and may have an adverse effect on the fish.

Biological Filtration: Bacteriological breakdown of toxic waste metabolites by the nitrification process is accomplished by bacteria of the genera *Nitrobacter* and *Nitrosomonas*. New aquariums must be seeded with these beneficial flora to avoid the accumulation of toxic levels of ammonia and nitrite. To seed the tank with these beneficial flora you can add a cup or two of gravel from an established tank filter if you're sure that the gravel-donating tank is free of infectious agents. If you're in doubt about the status of the tank, I suggest you purchase some cultured bacteria tablets such as Envirotrol-F® (Mardel Labs, Carol Stream, Illinois) or Nitro-Quik® (Hawaiian Marine Imports, Houston, Texas). If an Eheim power filter is used, this inoculum goes into the canister itself. Remember antibiotics can destroy these beneficial bacteria, which is another reason why you must have a separate treatment tank.

An effective mechanical filter is extremely important to your fishes' health. Notice that this Eheim power filter is placed below the water level of the aquarium. If the Eheim pump were above the water level you risk an air blockage in the impeller. There are many other pumps and filters available through your pet shop. Photo by Dr. Mark P. Dulin.

Mechanical Filtration: Decomposing particulate matter such as food, feces, and dead marine life must be removed, because it not only diminishes the oxygen level in the tank but also provides a favorable environment for excessive bacterial growth. Tank detritus can also lodge in the gill lamellae, thus inhibiting normal respiration.

Chemical Filtration: Activated charcoal is used to enhance the clarity of the tank and to adsorb dissolved chemicals and gases which may be toxic to fishes. Activated charcoal should be well washed and aged in salt water prior to use. The activated charcoal can also bind with therapeutic agents, which is one reason why you should not treat fishes in the exhibition tank. Drugs should not be used in the main tank even if you don't use activated charcoal or have discontinued filtration with charcoal during treatment.

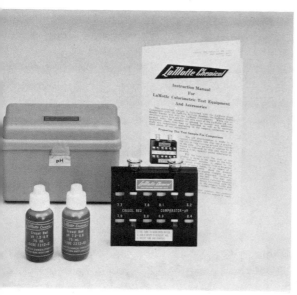

A variety of test kits are available for monitoring various water quality parameters in the *marine* aquarium. With a colorimetric pH test kit you can make a rapid and accurate determination of the pH in your marine aquarium. Photo courtesy of LaMotte Chemical Co.

pH Control: Natural sea water is alkaline, generally in the range of pH 8.2. If the pH gets out of balance, acidosis or alkalosis can result. Calcium carbonate (crushed sea shell) is often used in the tank bottom to help maintain the proper pH, as is dolomite.

This sick fish should be promptly removed from the exhibition tank, not only to avoid further spread of the disease, but also to prevent it from being attacked by healthy specimens. Photo by G. Marcuse.

Selection of Compatible Species: When you first stock your marine aquarium, the fishes will adapt to their surroundings easier if they are all put in together. Because they are all new to this environment they have not yet developed their territorial boundaries. Once a "peck order" is established, new arrivals may be treated harshly until new boundaries are set up. One way to reduce some of this territoriality prior to introducing new species is to give the fish a change of scenery by moving decorations around. In this way both the old and new fishes are presented with unfamiliar surroundings.

Generally it is unwise to put a "pair" of one particular fish species in the marine aquarium; this is especially true of angelfish species. My recommendation is to begin with hardy marine fishes such as damsels or blennies and make sure you consider species' compatibility when purchasing new fishes for your established tank. Aggressive behavior between incompatible species will result in injury and stress which will predispose the fishes to disease.

Ionic Content of the Water: Marine fishes cannot survive in a mixture of just water and sodium chloride. Many inorganic ions are necessary for life besides sodium and chloride. Many trace elements are also necessary for fish survival. Although I would not encourage you to make your own synthetic sea salt, I have listed the formula for the Cleveland modification of the Frankfurt formula. The amounts shown below will make 100 gallons at a specific gravity of 1.025.

Part I

NaCl	10.5	kg
$MgSO_4 \cdot 7H_2O$	2.62	kg
$MgCl \cdot 6H_2O$	2.04	kg
KCl	0.274	kg
$NaHCO_3$	0.079	kg
$SrCl_2 \cdot 6H_2O$	7.5	g
$MnSO_4 \cdot H_2O$	1.5	g
$Na_2HPO_4 \cdot 7H_2O$	1·25	g
LiCl	0.375	g
$Na_2MoO_4 \cdot 2H_2O$	0.375	g

Dissolve in warm water and keep fairly concentrated. Then add Part II and bring to specific gravity 1.025—around 100 gallons (US).

Part II

$CaCl_2$	0.52	kg

Dissolve in hot water and add to Part I.

Part III

KBr	270	g
Ca gluconate	6.25	g
KI	0.90	g

Dissolve in 2 liters of distilled water and add 80 ml per 100 gallons of Parts I plus II.

Part IV

$Al(SO_4)_3$	4.5	g
$CuSO_4 \cdot 5H_2O$	4.3	g
RbCl	1.5	g
$ZnSO_4 \cdot 7H_2O$	0.96	g
$CoSO_4$	0.50	g

Dissolve in 2 liters of distilled water and add 80 ml per 100 gallons of Parts I plus II after Part III has been added.

As you can see, it would be rather time-consuming to prepare your own synthetic sea water, and because non-polluted sea water is often difficult to obtain, most aquarists rely on a premixed synthetic salt water product. "Instant Ocean" (Aquarium Systems, Inc., East Lake, Ohio) is one such satisfactory sea salt mix. Many other satisfactory synthetic sea salt mixes, based upon the Frankfurt formula, are available at most tropical fish stores. Whichever brand of synthetic sea salt mix you use, make sure that you follow the manufacturer's instructions. Most aquarists use warm tap water to dissolve the salts more rapidly. Aerate the new salt-water vigorously for at least 24 hours to free the chlorine from the water and to provide the tank with a suitable dissolved oxygen level.

The acceptable range of salts is measured in terms of the specific gravity of the water. The instrument used to measure specific gravity is called a hydrometer. The most reliable hydrometers are those which have been standardized by the National Bureau of Standards.

Many hydrometers are sold within a cylindrical vessel which serves not only for storage but is also useful in checking the specific gravity. If you have such a container, add the aquarium water to the container, then put in the hydrometer to take a reading. If you don't have a cylindrical vessel, place the hydrometer directly into the aquarium itself, being careful to dislodge any bubbles which may become attached to the instrument. If it is necessary to shut off the aeration to obtain a smooth water surface, make sure you remember to turn the air back on after you have taken your reading. In either case, take the reading at the air-water interface (meniscus) *after* the instrument has stopped bobbing. The hydrometer will rise higher in saltier water, just as a swimmer floats easier in salt water than in fresh water.

Everyone knows that warm air is lighter than cold air, thus the rationale for hot-air balloons. Water acts in much the same manner; as you can see from the following table, water becomes less dense (lighter) as its temperature increases. Conversely, water becomes denser as its temperature decreases. Lucky for us, this holds true only to 4° C., at which point water again starts to become lighter; hence ice floats on water surfaces, approximately nine-tenths submerged.

The hydrometer reading should be taken periodically at the meniscus (air-water interface) and compared with the table of specific gravity values. If your tank is maintained at 76°-78° F (25° C), the reading should be 1.023. Photo by Dr. Herbert R. Axelrod.

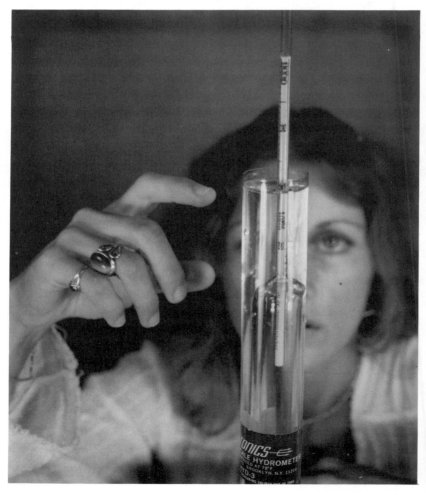

SPECIFIC GRAVITY VALUES OF SEA WATER
AT ITS MEAN SALINITY

Fahrenheit Temperature	Centigrade Temperature	Specific Gravity
86	30	1.021
84	29	1.021
82	28	1.022
81	27	1.022
79	26	1.022
77	25	1.023
75	24	1.023
73	23	1.023
72	22	1.023
70	21	1.024
68	20	1.024
66	19	1.024
64	18	1.025
63	17	1.025
61	16	1.025
59	15	1.025
57	14	1.025
55	13	1.026
54	12	1.026
52	11	1.026
50	10	1.026
48	9	1.026
46	8	1.027
45	7	1.027
43	6	1.027

Use the values from the table above for comparison with your tank's value at your tank's temperature. The difference in the two readings is how much the specific gravity of your tank needs to be corrected. The acceptable range is +0.002 from the proper value as shown on the table. If the specific gravity of your tank is higher, the water is too salty, so add tap water which has previously been aerated for 24 hours. Keep checking every hour and adding water until the correct specific gravity is obtained. If the specific gravity of your tank is lower, the water is too dilute, so remove the cover and allow evaporation to take place. Monitor the specific gravity daily until enough water has evaporated.

Keeping the specific gravity in the proper range is very important to the fishes' health. Without going into a big physiological discussion, I want to briefly describe how a bony marine fish survives in a salt water solution. Perhaps by knowing how the fish has come to survive in this seemingly unnatural solution you will be more conscientious about keeping the proper salinity in the aquarium.

Freshwater fishes are generally euryhaline, or salt-change tolerant. Marine fishes, on the other hand, are generally stenohaline, or relatively intolerant to salinity changes. Although there are some marine fishes which are less stenohaline than others, the exotic fishes you are likely to keep in your tank require a fairly constant salinity in the acceptable range.

Even though all the minerals in the Frankfurt formula are necessary for the fishes' health, they do make the salt water concentration hypertonic (higher in osmotic pressure) to the fluids within the fishes' bodies, just as the ocean does. Therefore, water tends to leave the fishes' membranes and salts tend to enter the fishes' membranes by simple osmosis. To counteract this water loss, exotic marine fishes drink sea water and eliminate their surplus salts through the gills and in the feces. Only trace amounts leave through the urine. Eliminating these salts across the gill membranes is an active process and thus requires energy. Whenever the salinity deviates much from that of normal sea water, you are putting unnecessary stress on the fish.

Significant salinity deviations can result in the outright death of the fish. Subtle salinity deviations stress the fish, and stress predisposes the fish to acquiring disease.

The above items are the main environmental factors which must be considered when setting up a marine aquarium. The various water quality parameters should be monitored and corrected as needed to assure a proper environment for exotic marine fishes.

Fish Anatomy

You must become familiar with normal fish appearance before expecting to recognize the abnormal. Once familiar with normal coloration, fin integrity, morphology, and other anatomical features you should readily recognize when an abnormality occurs. The accompanying line drawings demonstrate both external and internal anatomical features.

STRUCTURE OF THE GILL

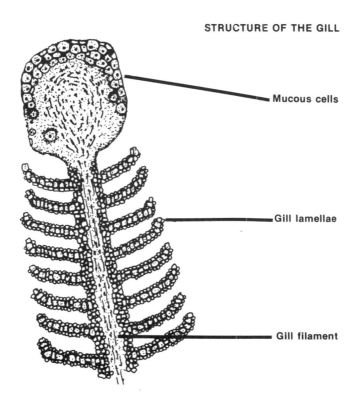

Mucous cells

Gill lamellae

Gill filament

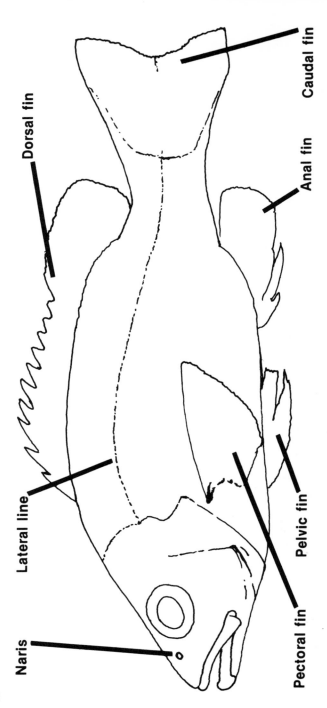

EXTERNAL ANATOMY OF A TYPICAL MARINE FISH

Dorsal fin

Caudal fin

Anal fin

Lateral line

Pelvic fin

Pectoral fin

Naris

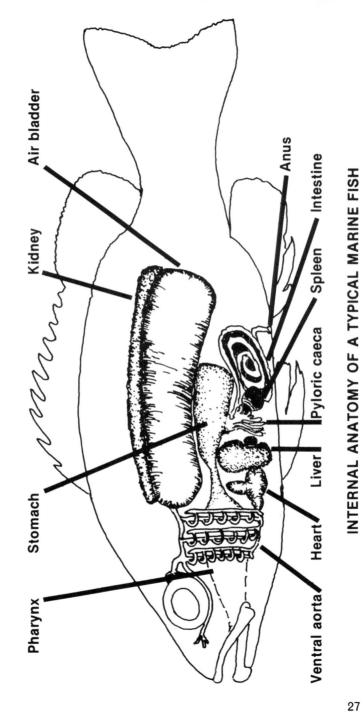

INTERNAL ANATOMY OF A TYPICAL MARINE FISH

Air bladder

Anus

Intestine

Kidney

Spleen

Stomach

Pyloric caeca

Liver

Heart

Pharynx

Ventral aorta

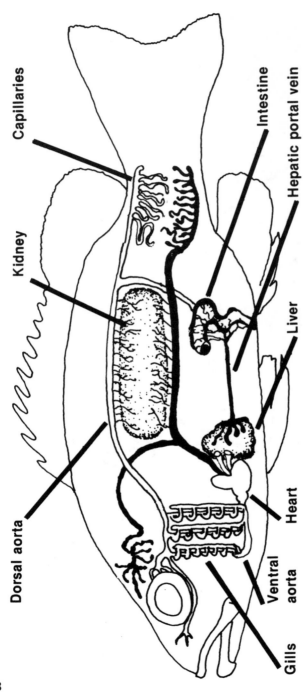

Capillaries

Intestine

Hepatic portal vein

Kidney

Liver

Dorsal aorta

Heart

Ventral aorta

Gills

BLOOD CIRCULATION OF A TYPICAL MARINE FISH

A typical fish skeleton. Photo courtesy American Museum of Natural History.

Knowing the normal appearance and anatomical features of the particular fishes which you are keeping cannot be emphasized too strongly. These fishes should be examined closely prior to acquisition and their coloration, scale, fin, and skin appearance carefully noted.

In order to become familiar with fish anatomy you should dissect some fish when the opportunity arises. You won't be able to recognize abnormal tissue unless you first know what normal tissue looks like. Photo by Dr. Herbert R. Axelrod.

Epidemiology of Disease

Clinically healthy fish may be "infected" with potentially pathogenic organisms yet show no clinical signs of being diseased. "Infection" means that the organism is residing in or on the host; it does not mean that a diseased state exists. Asymptomatic "carrier" fishes can harbor pathogenic organisms without any adverse effects until a stress situation develops. As is the case with any other animal, stress predisposes the individual to disease.

Disease is the antithesis of health. There are internal and external diseases, organic and functional diseases, developmental abnormalities, degenerative diseases, and deficiency diseases. More specifically, there are diseases caused by viruses, fungi, bacteria, protozoans, worms, and crustaceans, as well as diseases caused by the artificial environment of captivity itself, such as metal and gaseous poisoning. . . even poisoning by algae!

Epizootics may be caused in tanks by pathogens which are present in the wild but which do not reach any significant proportions there. *Oodinium*, a parasitic dinoflagellate, is one example, and *Cryptocaryon*, a ciliated protozoan, is another.

A general reason for this higher incidence of disease in captivity is the greatly decreased ratio of fishes to volume of water; more specifically, (1) greater transmission occurs in the tank due to closer contact among fishes, (2) increased chances of temperature, ammonia, nitrite, pH, salinity, and oxygen fluctuations, (3) dietary inadequacies leading to lowered resistance to infectious organisms already present, (4) shorter generation periods for those organisms, and (5) absence of natural predators in the tank, thus providing diseased individuals a better chance of survival.

Diseases can be either infectious or noninfectious. Infectious diseases are caused by organisms whereas noninfectious diseases are caused by physical anomalies, adverse environmental conditions, or wounds. By definition, when a diseased state exists, characteristic clinical signs and pathological changes occur. Once you have recognized the particular disease, appropriate treatment can be initiated.

A *Pomacanthus semicirculatus* showing obvious signs of disease should not be placed in the exhibition tank. It should be quarantined and treated until ALL clinical signs of disease are gone. Photo by G. Marcuse.

Probably one of the most important and yet most overlooked areas of aquatic animal medicine is epidemiology. Epidemiology is that science which deals with the incidence, distribution, and control of disease in a population. If you have a firm grasp of epidemiological principles, many disease outbreaks can be avoided.

Rarely does an aquarist obtain all the fishes, invertebrates, and ornamental shells and corals from a selected ocean site. If everything in the tank was obtained from one area, the fishes would likely have some degree of immunity to diseases which are endemic to that location. Generally the fishes and invertebrates you put into your tank come from a variety of locations throughout the tropical areas of the world. Some of your blennies may have had previous exposure to an *Aeromonas* species and developed a degree of natural resistance to these bacteria. Others may never have been exposed, and putting these *Aeromonas*-unexposed blennies with fishes (or invertebrates) harboring the organism may lead to a disease condition. Many factors are involved in whether or not the unexposed blennies will actually become sick. If they are healthy and the number of pathogenic bacteria they are exposed to is small, their natural body defenses may control the *Aeromonas* infection and a state of immunity may develop. On the other hand, if your previously unexposed blennies are debilitated or suffering from stress when you put in "carrier" fishes or invertebrates, a diseased state will probably develop.

Many factors influence whether or not this type of situation will result in overt disease. These include such factors as (1) species susceptibility, (2) numbers of organisms which are in contact with the fish, (3) degree of immunogenicity, (4) degree of virulence of the pathogen, and (5) environmental factors.

If the environmental conditions are stressful to the fishes, the pendulum will swing in favor of bacterial invasion. If the bacteria multiply in the aquarium water, as is the case with aquatic saprophytes, the fishes can be exposed to tremendous loads of the organism at once. When the critical mass becomes large enough, the fishes' protective

Invertebrates such as the sea anemone (*Condylactis passiflora*) or the Hawaiian red shrimp may introduce pathogenic organisms into your tank. They should, therefore, be quarantined in the same manner as new fishes. Upper photo by U. Erich Friese; lower photo by A. Norman.

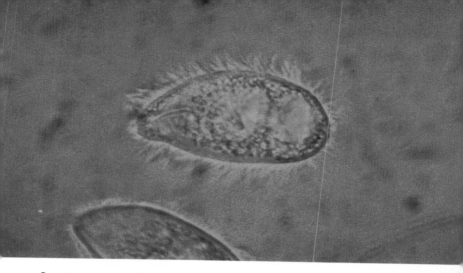

Cryptocaryon irritans can cause white spot disease in marine fishes. These organisms can be introduced not only by fishes and invertebrates but also by ornamental shells recently removed from the ocean. Photo by Drs. R. Nigrelli and G.D. Ruggieri, Osborne Lab., New York Aquarium.

To avoid introducing disease causing organisms, decorative shells should be cleaned and disinfected prior to placing them in the exhibition tank.

mechanism may be overwhelmed, and clinical signs of an acute disease may develop. My intention is not to go into great detail on bacteriology but merely to make you aware that many factors and variables exist in the disease process. By knowing these concepts, costly mistakes can be avoided.

What can you; the aquarist, do to reduce the likelihood of creating an epizootic in your aquarium? First, consider every object you put into your tank to be contaminated with potentially pathogenic organisms. You can introduce these organisms into your aquarium via new fishes,

Coral is often used to decorate marine aquariums. Make sure all non-living objects (fomites) are thoroughly cleaned and rinsed prior to putting them into your marine exhibition tank. Photo by Robert Straughan.

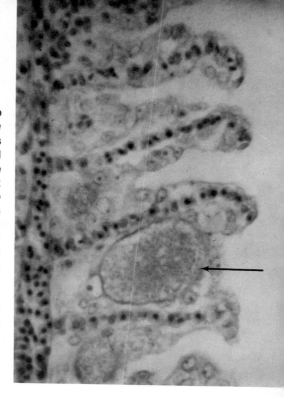

This magnified photo of *Oodinium ocellatum* shows its attachment to the gill lamellae of a marine fish. An alert aquarist will be able to diagnose early stages of oodinosis based on rapid breathing and discomfort of the fish. Copper sulfate therapy of new arrivals in the quarantine tank could prevent an epizootic of marine "ich" or white spot disease in the exhibition tank. Photo by Frickhinger.

invertebrates, plants, live or unprocessed food, your fingers, and even such inanimate objects as seashells. I realize it would be tempting to add your newly acquired gorgonians directly to the tank—but first consider the possible consequences. Although this gorgonian is probably not "infected" with *Oodinium*, it could very well be harboring the pathogen. In addition to harboring *Oodinium*, your gorgonian could also harbor *Cryptocaryon irritans*. Why risk an outbreak of white spot disease in your aquarium? Quarantine and treat the gorgonian prior to putting it into your tank. A 2- to 3-week quarantine with several 3- to 5-minute freshwater baths will render the gorgonian (and other invertebrates) free of both *Oodinium* and *Cryptocaryon*. To be on the safe side, consider a 2- to 3-week quarantine necessary for *all* incoming fishes and invertebrates and a disinfection process (such as boiling) necessary for all non-living ornamental aquarium objects.

In the early stages of white spot disease, caused either by *Crypto-caryon* or *Oodinium,* the clinical signs will include rapid breathing, scraping the opercle on objects, and "flashing" or rapid erratic movements. Photo by Dr. Herbert R. Axelrod.

In the later stages of white spot disease, large patches occur on the fish's body. The aquarist should not allow the disease to progress to this stage before beginning copper sulfate therapy. Photo by Frickhinger.

Impexus, a parasitic copepod, has attached itself to a highly vascular area of this firefish's body. Photo by Dr. K.H. Choo.

Single copepods, like this one, can be surgically dissected from the fish. When an insecticide such as Dylox® is used, the head of the copepod can remain on the fish and leave an unsightly scar. Photo by G.C. Blasiola, Jr.

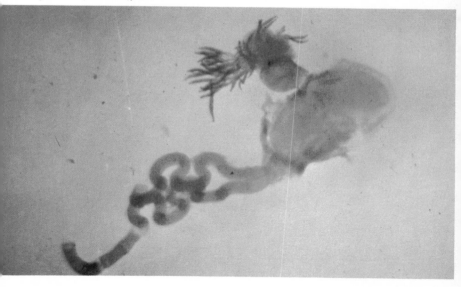

I will describe how to maintain and treat "newcomers" in a quarantine/treatment tank later; for now just concern yourself with why this quarantine step is necessary. Epidemiologically speaking, the aquarist should be concerned with all possible sources of infection, modes of transmission of these infectious agents, and the various routes of entry of these organisms. Sources of aquarium infection include both symptomatic and asymptomatic carrier fishes. "Convalescent" carrier fishes have clinically recovered from the disease but still harbor the organism. "Chronically infected" carriers are sick fishes which shed the organism on a continuous or intermittent basis. "Healthy" carriers (asymptomatics) are healthy fishes which excrete the organism, thereby serving as a potential source of infection to the rest of the population. In addition to new fishes that can bring in the organism, invertebrates, plants, and fomites (inanimate contaminated objects) can also carry disease-causing organisms.

Fomites, such as this net, can spread disease from one tank to another. You should use a separate net for each tank or disinfect it after each use.

The lionfish (above) displays its fins in the normal manner while the same fish (in the photo below) shows a clinical sign of disease by folding all its fin. Photos by G. Budich.

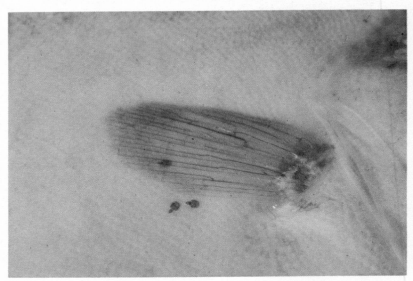

The reddened fin has been attacked by several parasitic copepods. The female parasite shown enlarged in the photo below is capable of causing extensive damage to the fish's skin. Photos by Dr. R. Pulin and Mr. C. Bridge.

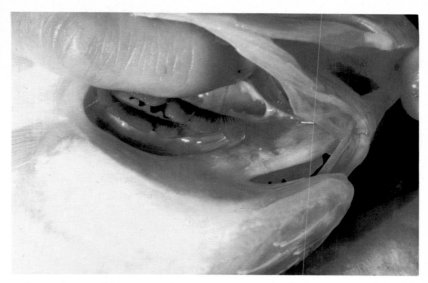

Several parasitic copepods are seen near the fish's gills. The adult female and juvenile (shown enlarged below) could be removed by hand. If the tank is infested with these parasites, the fish will need to be quarantined and treated until a "die-off" of infective stages occurs. Photos by Dr. R. Pulin and Mr. C. Bridge.

Invertebrates can introduce disease into an exhibition tank. They should be given freshwater baths and quarantined in the same manner in which new arrivals of fish are treated. Copper sulfate therapy is too toxic to be given to invertebrates. Photo courtesy of Aquarium Systems, Inc.

Aquarium fishes have several modes of transmission of infectious agents. Fish-to-fish transmission is most common with water acting as the vehicle of transmission. Sick fishes can shed pathogens via wounds or feces or by dying and undergoing decomposition within the tank. As they decompose, pathogenic organisms can be released into the water. Unless a fish eats all or part of the sick fish (or a parasite which has recently fed on this sick fish), the vehicle of transmission is the aquarium water itself.

Pathogenic organisms can enter a fish's body in a variety of ways. The most common route of entry is probably by absorption or penetration of the gut lining. Bacteria can also enter the fish via transgressing the gill lamellae or by invading injured skin.

Ideally, it would be best to know exactly what (if any) infection the "newcomers" had, the life cycle of this organism, and the preferred method of treatment. Because you, as a tropical fish hobbyist, would not find it desirable to sacrifice a statistically significant number of your new acquisitions and have them screened for various infectious diseases, let's be unjust and assume your newcomers are "guilty until proved innocent." No harm will come to them if the quarantine/treatment procedure is done properly, and your established aquarium fishes will live a longer life because of your new epidemiological perspective.

Methods of Disease Prevention

ENVIRONMENTAL FACTORS

If you can provide your fishes with optimum environmental conditions and adequate nutrition, your disease outbreaks will likely be minimal. Maintaining health with preventive medicine has always been more successful than treating infectious diseases with drugs. To use an old adage, "an ounce of prevention is worth a pound of cure." Providing your fishes with an optimum environment, however, is not an easy task and involves a basic understanding of a diverse group of principles. Not only must you maintain proper water quality parameters, but also you need to avoid the introduction of toxins and pathogenic organisms. Stress should be avoided, and this involves a multitude of factors such as stocking your tank only with compatible species and providing your fishes with proper nutrition. I want to whet your appetite with some of the basic environmental considerations; if you are not familiar with these concepts, you should consult more detailed reference material.

Providing your fishes with an optimum environment requires monitoring water chemistries and making corrective changes when they are indicated. Aquarium instruments and kits are available for checking pH, salt content (specific gravity), temperature, ammonia and nitrite levels, dissolved oxygen, and a variety of other factors. Whether or not you need to monitor all these parameters depends on your experience and particular aquarium situation.

To minimize the likelihood of toxic effects from metabolic waste byproducts, **the tank must not be overcrowded.** The amount of animal life an aquarium can safely hold is its *carrying capacity*. The carrying capacity of marine tanks is considerably less than that of freshwater aquariums. Tank

Overcrowding and close contact of fishes can lead to the accumulation of toxic waste products and the easy transfer of parasites. Make sure you don't exceed the carrying capacity of your tank. Photo by F. Yasuda.

Copepods, as shown in this enlargement, have attached themselves to the gill filaments. These parasites can damage the gills and predispose the fish to secondary bacterial invasion and heavy infestations can make the fish anemic. Photo by Dr. Mark P. Dulin.

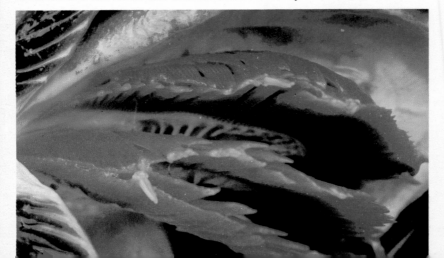

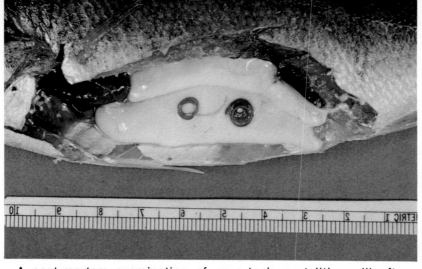

A post-mortem examination of your tank mortalities will often reveal pathological changes which will be of value in treating the surviving fish. This fish has nematode (roundworm) parasitism. Photo by Dr. Decktiarenko.

The swim bladder of this fish is heavily parasitized with round-worms. Photo by Dr. P. de Kinkelin.

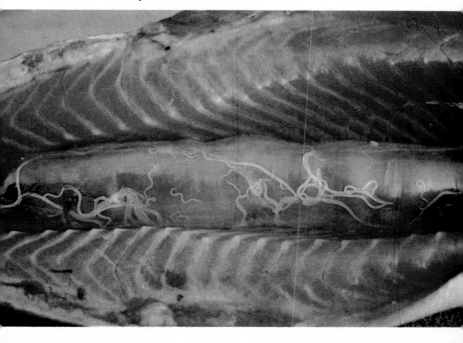

size is not the only factor to consider in determining carrying capacity. You must also consider such things as the turnover rate (circulation time), the cubic filter bed space, the grain size of the filter medium, the territoriality of the fish species, and the amount of food you put in the tank. If you are not familiar with the carrying capacity of your particular aquarium set-up, consult a good marine aquarium text or a marine aquarist at a reliable tropical fish store. *Exotic Marine Fishes* and *The Marine Aquarium in Theory and Practice* are two excellent texts with extensive coverage of topics dealing with the set-up and maintenance of marine aquaria.

NUTRITION

Because of the highly diverse environment which they inhabit, fishes—marine fishes in particular—have developed many evolutionary changes to favor survival. To avoid direct competition, many marine fishes have developed a very specialized mode of life. By occupying a specific ecological niche, these fishes can often avoid direct competition with other specialized fishes. These specific "ecological niches" of marine life are energized by a variety of types of food. There are carnivorous, herbivorous, and omnivorous fishes; there are fishes which filter plankton with their gill rakers, fishes that feed on detritus, and fishes which are voracious predators. There are benthic feeders, pelagic feeders, and fishes which have evolved to feed directly from the water surface.

Knowledge of the dietary requirements of many fish species is based on observations of their eating habits in the wild, examination of the wild fishes' stomach contents, and using an experimental approach to feeding these species in captivity. By these means, various dietary formulations have been developed by a number of commercial firms.

I would be suspicious of any prepared food which claims to provide all your fishes with 100% adequate nutrition. Vitamins are fragile compounds, and it is therefore not likely that a dried flake food which has set on the shelf for any period of time would contain adequate vitamin levels. Protein levels can also be deceiving—just because a product boasts of a high protein level does not mean that it necessarily has the proper proportion of available essential amino acids. My recommendation is to play it safe and provide your fishes with a *variety* of natural and prepared foods. By natural foods I am referring to animal and plant tissues in either the live, fresh, or frozen state.

Raw shrimp and frozen non-oily fishes are excellent sources of protein and should be fed to your fishes on a routine basis. Shrimp and fillets can be kept frozen and small portions sliced off and thawed prior to feeding; pet shops generally sell an excellent variety of frozen foods.

This sea horse has successfully obtained a shrimp dinner. Cultured live shrimp can provide your fishes with a fresh supply of vitamins in addition to many of the essential amino acids. There is no substitute for live food. Photo by H. Hansen.

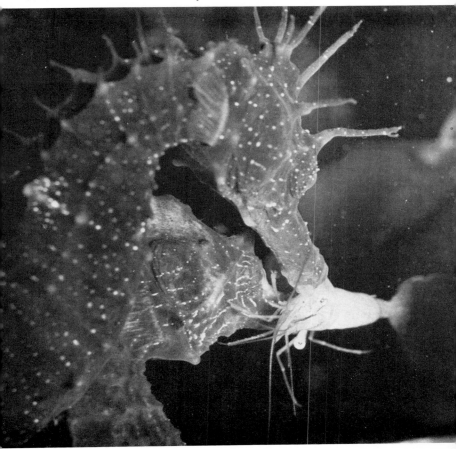

Edible mussels can be found on most coastal shorelines; however, these fresh live foods have the potential to introduce pathogenic organisms. To play it safe scald them before putting them into your tank. Photo by Dr. K. Knaack.

Pet stores offer a wide selection of frozen fish food products. To insure your fishes are getting all the essential nutrients it is best to feed a variety of food.

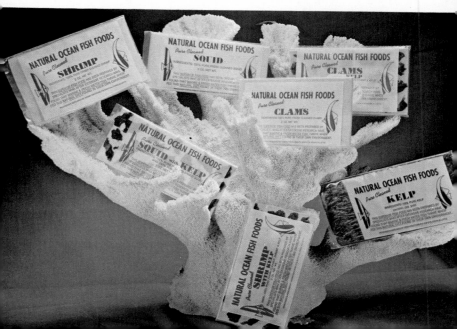

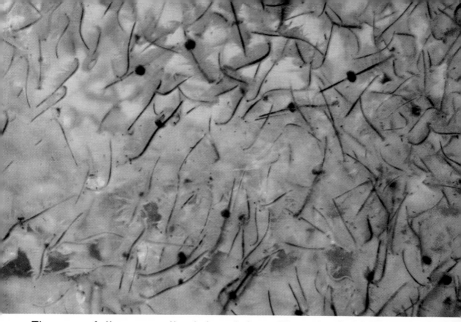

These are fully grown live brine shrimp. Photo by C. Masters.

Scallops are filter feeders and should be fed fine food such as brine shrimp. To insure ample food is directed toward them many aquarists aim the food at them with a large pipette and suction bulb. Photo by Dr.. Herbert R. Axelrod.

Brine shrimp and spinach should also be fed on a periodic basis. If you are using the frozen products, don't get lazy and throw a big slab of frozen brine shrimp into the tank. You should thaw it in a glass of tap water, allow it to settle, pour off the water, rinse it again and then drain prior to feeding.

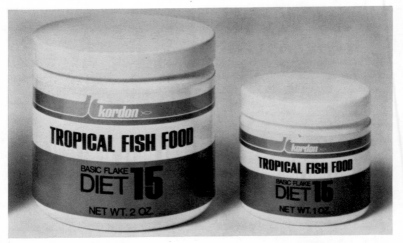

There are many brands of flake food available at pet shops. Quality flake foods can provide an excellent supplement to your fish's dietary needs.

Live foods are the most desirable source of food for your fishes as long as pathogenic organisms are not introduced by these foods. Although cultured living animals (such as brine shrimp, white worms, tubifex worms, and earthworms) may be fed to marine fishes, you should not feed marine fishes with organisms captured in the wild. You can bend this rule a little and feed the musculature from larger healthy fishes, shrimp, or lobsters, but don't feed entire invertebrate animals or plants you might find. Freezing wild-caught food items will not necessarily render them free of infectious agents. Wild food can introduce pathogenic organisms, so play it safe and don't use them.

Live foods, like cultured brine shrimp and earthworms, are especially valuable in providing your fishes with vitamins. The vitamins in living organisms have not been previously destroyed by drying, nor will they dissipate into the water as can happen with prepared foods.

How and when you feed is almost as important as what you feed. Small species should receive frequent feedings of small amounts throughout the day. You have subjected your fishes to an artificial environment, so you cannot just pour in the food and expect the small and weak to survive. Dominance and competition for food are a part of this unnatural habitat. It will be up to you to provide each fish (and invertebrate) with its fair share. In some tank situations a pipette and suction bulb is required to "aim" the food at the smaller fish.

Young children love to feed fish, but close supervision is often necessary. Dumping in a heavy load of food can overload the biological filter and stress the fishes. I will never forget the time my son dumped in an entire box of Cheerios to feed his favorite pets—fortunately Cheerios float.

Malnutrition predisposes animals to disease. By providing your fishes with a balanced diet, the normal body defenses are more likely to function properly and the fish will be less susceptible to infectious agents.

TREATMENT AND QUARANTINE OF NEW SPECIES

A 2- to 3-week quarantine period should be considered essential for all newly acquired fishes and invertebrates even if they have undergone previous quarantine and treatment at the dealer's shop. A separate quarantine/treatment tank should be considered essential for the serious marine aquarist. This tank does not need to be elaborate; in fact, it should be very simple. I recommend the use of a bare all-glass aquarium because plastic containers can adsorb some of the therapeutic agents you will likely be using. A residual amount of one drug can often counteract the effectiveness of another drug, and in some cases a combination of therapeutic agents can result in the formation of a poison, as is the case with a formalin/methylene blue combination.

Consider a 10- to 20-gallon glass quarantine/treatment tank to be a small investment, considering that it may prevent you from losing your entire exhibition tank. Later in

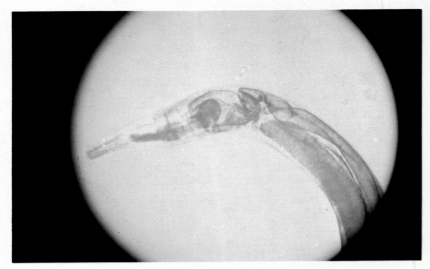

Adult nematodes such as this one are common in the digestive tract of marine fishes. Many fishes can be infected for years without showing any clinical signs of disease. Photo by Dr. Jim Chacko.

When migrating stages of parasitic worms invade body organs, clinical signs of disease may occur. These parasitic capsules in the liver have destroyed a good portion of the liver tissue. Photo by Dr. J. Chubb.

Acanthocephalans can cause severe damage to the intestinal wall. In the upper photo the proboscis of a thorny-headed worm is extended; in the photo below the proboscis is retracted. Acanthocephalans can be removed by treating the fish with food impregnated with piperazine. Photo by Dr. J.C. Chubb.

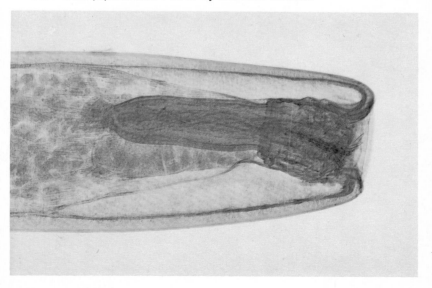

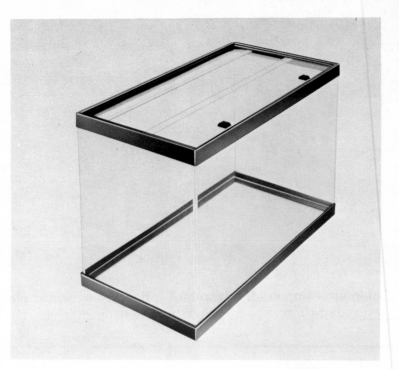

A bare all glass quarantine/treatment tank should be kept ready for new arrivals or emergency conditions. The water in this tank should have the same pH, temperature, and salinity as the exhibition tank and should be aerated constantly.

this manual I will list specific doses of therapeutic agents to add to this tank, such as 1 ml (20 drops) per gallon of tank water. It is therefore essential to know exactly how many gallons are in the tank at the time of treatment. The gallon tank capacity can be calculated by the following formula (inside dimensions):

$$\frac{\text{Length X Width X Heighth (in inches)}}{231} = \begin{array}{l}\text{capacity in} \\ \text{American gallons}\end{array}$$

Because you need to mix the synthetic sea salt with the exact amount of water, I suggest you measure your tank's capacity the first time by counting the gallon bottles of water you pour in. Mark the tank at the top of this known level with its gallon capacity by using adhesive labels or some other permanent reminder.

This is very important, because an advertised 20-gallon aquarium does not usually hold 20 gallons. You must know exactly how much water is in the tank so that you can add the *correct* dose of treatment solutions. When evaporation occurs you know exactly how much water to add to fill the tank back to its known gallon capacity.

After each quarantine or treatment period the tank should be thoroughly washed, disinfected, and rinsed. Many disinfecting solutions are available such as the iodophors (Betadine® , Wescodyne®), or the quarternary ammonium compounds (Hyamine® , Roccal®), or just plain everyday Clorox® . After washing and disinfection, rinse the tank *thoroughly* prior to restocking with artificial sea water. The tank should be aerated vigorously for 24 hours prior to the admission of newcomers to make sure all residual chlorine is gone and to ensure an adequate level of dissolved oxygen. A filtration system is not necessary or desirable in this tank. The therapeutic agents you will be using would either kill off the beneficial bacterial flora or become adsorbed to the activated charcoal. Because you will be changing the water frequently, a 20-gallon tank is large enough for small numbers of newcomers without worrying about metabolic waste byproduct buildup. This tank should also have a cover, as some of these treatments may provoke the fish into jumping out!

METHOD OF TREATMENT

1) The tank should contain artificial sea water and be aerated 24 hours prior to the admission of newcomers.
2) The temperature, salinity, and pH of the quarantine tank should be equalized to that of the water in which the fishes (or invertebrates) have been received. Ask your

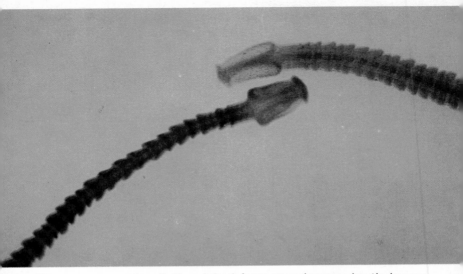

Tapeworms can be distinguished from roundworms by their conspicuous reproductive segments (proglottids). Photo by Dr. L. Margolis.

Adult tapeworms can be removed from the intestinal tract by feeding the fish food impregnated with Yomesan® . Photo by T.H. Wellborn.

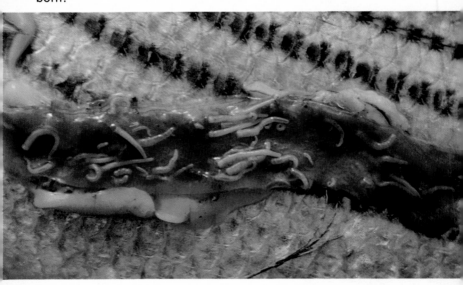

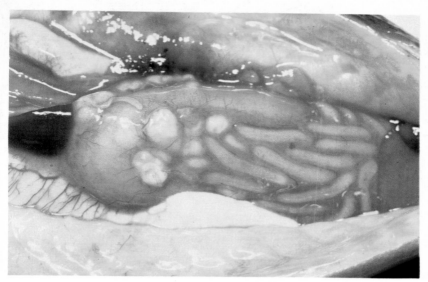

The migrating parasitic stages of a fish tapeworm have invaded the stomach wall of this fish thereby reducing the effectiveness of the digestive process. Photo by Dr. J. Chubb.

This magnified histologic section of the stomach tissue shows a transverse section of the migrating stage of the fish tapeworm. Photo by Dr. J. Chubb.

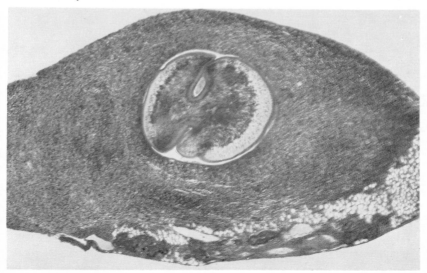

59

dealer what the specific gravity reading was in the tank from which your fish was removed.

3) Transfer the specimens to the quarantine tank and withhold all food. Set up a freshwater bath. A one-gallon wide-mouth glass bottle will work for small specimens. Fill the container with tap water and aerate vigorously for 24 hours. This will provide a suitable dissolved oxygen level and rid the water of chlorine. Make sure the temperature and pH are the same as the quarantine tank. Tap water generally will be more acidic than the salt water solution, so sodium bicarbonate (baking soda) should be added to make the pH more alkaline.

4) Net the specimen(s) from the quarantine tank after 24 hours and place them into the freshwater bath for 3 minutes, then return them to the quarantine tank. By virtue of the osmotic pressure differential, this freshwater bath will generally cause ectoparasites to fall off and will rupture the cells of dinoflagellates such as *Oodinium*. This is a safe procedure for both fishes and invertebrates. Most of these species can withstand an abrupt change in hydrostatic pressure for 10 to 30 minutes without suffering from any long-term side effects. Temporary incoordination may result, but unless a fish or invertebrate shows signs of severe distress, leave it in the bath for the full 3 minutes.

5) A small amount of food can be given to the fish after a short readjustment period in the quarantine tank.

6) Throughout the next 12 to 19 days of quarantine, feed the fishes and/or invertebrates sparingly and observe them closely. If any of the clinical signs of disease erupt, stop feeding and begin appropriate treatments as covered in the diagnosis and treatment section. There is no biological filtration in this quarantine/treatment tank, so the ammonia-nitrogen level should be monitored; if high levels develop, a water change must be made.

Some fish disease experts recommend the prophylactic use of broad-spectrum antibiotics as part of the routine quarantine procedure. Although I don't think this is a bad idea, I do feel that it is unlikely that the average saltwater aquarist would go to the trouble and expense to treat fishes for an infectious condition which might not exist. If you are a serious aquarist with a considerable economic investment in your exhibition tank, you may want to take this precautionary step and treat all incoming fishes as though they harbor potential pathogens.

I don't want to give the impression that a broad-spectrum antibiotic treatment is a panacea capable of freeing your fishes of all potentially pathogenic organisms. Not all bacteria are susceptible to a broad-spectrum antibiotic, and even some bacteria that are normally susceptible may be "walled-off" in various organs of the carrier fish. These

Even this healthy-looking *Zebrasoma scopas* could harbor potentially pathogenic organisms. It should therefore be quarantined and observed for the development of clinical signs of disease prior to placing it in the exhibition tank. Photo by G. Marcuse.

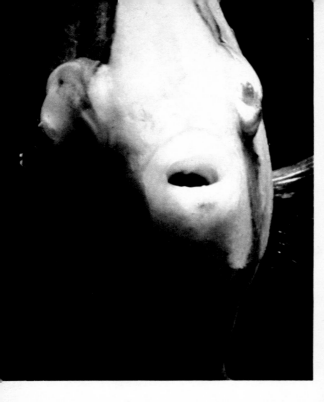

Exophthalmos (pop-eye) is not pathognomonic of one particular disease. A variety of infectious and non-infectious diseases can lead to this clinical sign of disease. Photo by Dr. H. Reichenbach-Klinke.

Below: Parasitic cysts can occur externally as well as internally. This cyst would eventually rupture, freeing infective stages of the parasite. Photo by Dr. Mawdesley-Thomas.

Bilateral exophthalmia (pop-eyes), plus ascites (swollen abdomen from the accumulation of body fluids) is often seen in kidney disease. Photo by Dr. Mark P. Dulin.

Removing the cranium to expose the brain should be completed on all post-mortem examinations. The meningitis seen on this fish is often observed in acute systemic bacterial infections. Photo by Dr. Mark P. Dulin.

pathogens could later escape these fibrotic nodule "hiding places" during a subsequent stressful or debilitated condition. A properly administered broad-spectrum antibiotic course of therapy could probably clear up the majority of the commonly occurring bacterial infections in the carrier state and should therefore be considered as a plausable step in the quarantine procedure. I suspect that those who are interested in this prophylactic procedure are familiar with, and have access to, a variety of antibacterial agents. I would encourage you *not* to use oxytetracycline (Terramycin®), the penicillins, or sulfa drugs as your broad-spectrum antibiotics of choice. Because of their long-term, low-dose usage among aquarists, most fish disease pathogens have developed some resistance to them. This development of drug-resistant strains is a good example of why continuous low-level dosage of drugs is not a good idea. Whenever antibiotics are used, they should be used in the full recommended strength over the recommended period of time, otherwise you simply select for a more resistant strain of bacteria.

If you are inclined to treat fishes before the development of clinical signs of disease, I suggest the use of the following water-soluble broad-spectrum antibiotics:

Chloramphenicol sodium succinate (Chloromycetin®),
Gentamicin sulfate (Garamycin®),
Kanamycin sulfate (Kantrex®), or
Neomycin sulfate.

I have listed the dosage for an antibacterial treatment with these therapeutic agents in the diagnosis and treatment section of this book.

I want to emphasize that although many parasitic organisms will not survive this quarantine period and freshwater bath, the main purpose of the quarantine is to observe the fish and have it isolated in case clinical signs of disease occur. This isolation will not only protect the fishes in the exhibition tank from pathogen exposure but also allows for easy treatment of an already quarantined fish. Further stressing an already sick fish by capture and tank transfer is not necessary.

Post-Mortem Examination

I want to encourage you to get into the habit of conducting a post-mortem examination on your tank mortalities. The necropsy, or post-mortem procedure, can be extremely valuable in determining the cause of death, and unless you have a good idea of why a particular fish died, future deaths may occur.

Only recent mortalities are valuable for a necropsy procedure. Tropical fishes will rapidly undergo decomposition in a warm tank, and these post-mortem changes can interfere with a proper diagnosis. If you cannot examine the dead fishes shortly after death, refrigerate them for later examination. Generally, it is best to necropsy the fish upon discovery; bagging it in the refrigerator only leads to procrastination and will delay your knowing the cause of death. Other fishes may soon show clinical signs of the same disease, and unless you know why a given fish died, you are not likely to know how to treat your surviving fishes.

Only a few instruments are needed for a standard necropsy procedure. If a scalpel, iris scissors, and fine-pointed thumb forceps are not readily available, a single-edged razor blade, manicure scissors, and household tweezers will suffice. If you have access to a microscope, by all means use it to your advantage. A dissection microscope is especially valuable for small specimens. If you are not lucky enough to have a microscope, use an ordinary magnifying lens to help you detect gill and external parasites.

It is practically impossible to obtain a definitive diagnosis based upon gross examination of a single fish lesion, but a combination of clinical signs of disease and gross pathological changes throughout various organs can often render a fairly specific diagnosis. Remember, we are only

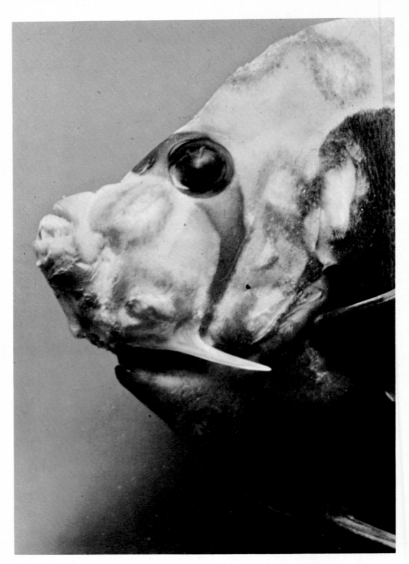

Severe erosion and inflammation of this fish's head are indicative of an acute bacterial infection. This fish should be placed in the treatment tank and given a broad spectrum antibiotic treatment for 5 to 7 days. It is possible to cure this fish. Photo by Frickhinger.

The extreme reddening and swelling of the abdominal tissues of this fish are indicative of an acute systemic bacterial infection. A broad spectrum antibiotic, such as Chloromycetin, gentamycin, or kanamycin, should bring about a cure to infectious bacterial diseases such as this. Photo by Dr. Mark P. Dulin.

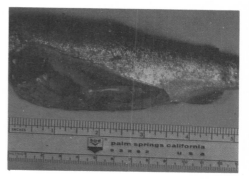

When a bacterial infection has progressed to the stage shown here, fungus often invades the dead tissues. Amputation of the distal (end) portion of the tail fin, plus antibiotic therapy, resulted in the regeneration of this tail.

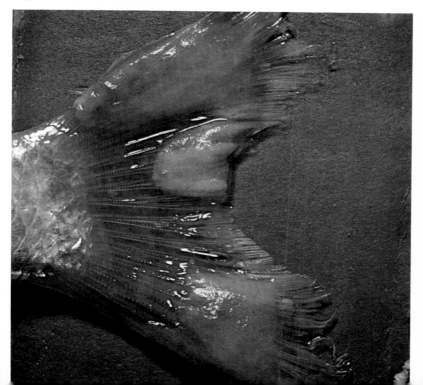

concerned with getting the diagnosis to a level at which appropriate treatment can be instituted. Don't concern yourself with which particular ciliated protozoan is causing gill pathology, since appropriate measures can be initiated by just knowing the treatment for an external protozoan infection.

Do the necropsy carefully and record the findings in a notebook. If you have close-up photographic capabilities, you have an excellent means of keeping a record of your disease problems. Color transparencies (slides) are also useful if you have an unusual disease condition and need to send a description and samples to a fish disease expert.

Don't settle for finding one pathological change and jumping to any immediate conclusions. Few fish diseases leave a single outstanding lesion which can be considered pathognomonic for that particular disease. A combination of clinical signs and various pathological changes, however, can often lead to a proper diagnosis. For example, let us assume you just noticed your favorite clown fish go belly-up and take its last gasp of air. Even though you are tired and had just settled back with your favorite music, you (being the conscientious aquarist that you are) jump up and remove your dead pet. Rather than grieve over the loss and flush it down the toilet, you set forth on your first necropsy procedure. After placing the fish on a damp paper towel and grabbing your scissors, tweezers, and blade you are ready to begin dissecting. But wait, take a close look at the external anatomy first. Is everything normal, or are the fins frayed and one eye protruding? Say you only notice unilateral exophthalmos (one-sided pop-eye). Are you going to quit there, jump to the conclusion it died of T.B., and go back to your music? No! You are an inquisitive scientist, and you are going to thoroughly check out every possibility within your capabilities.

What caused this eye to protrude? Was it from gas bubble disease? Although gas bubble disease occurs in marine fishes below hydroelectric dams, its appearance would be extremely unlikely in a warm-water marine aquarium. Perhaps an increase in intraocular pressure

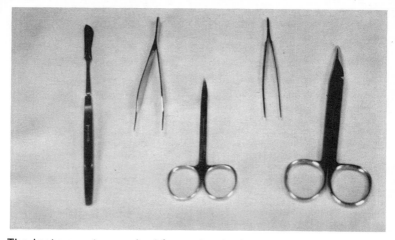

The instruments *required* for a standard necropsy (post-mortem) procedure are a scalpel, forceps and scissors. If you don't have these instruments then a single edged razor blade, tweezers, and manicure scissors will suffice.

caused this eye to protrude? Some systemic bacterial pathogens can multiply and do damage within the vitreous of the eye itself. Others can multiply behind the eye, and the subsequent inflammatory reaction can cause the eye to protrude. If a systemic bacterial infection caused this clinical manifestation of disease, pathological changes should be seen elsewhere; perhaps you overlooked the reddening and fraying of the fins. These signs indicate a loss of capillary and tissue integrity, which often occurs in a systemic bacterial disease.

Or perhaps the swollen eye has been caused by a build-up of body fluids, which often happens during renal (kidney) failure. If this is the case, other pathological signs of disease will likely be apparent, such as a swollen abdomen due to ascites (accumulation of fluids within the abdominal cavity). If you failed to notice the ascites from the external examination, you surely would have picked it up on your internal examination. Your initial midline incision would likely have brought forth a gush of free fluid from the abdomen. If the exophthalmos is indeed a clinical mani-

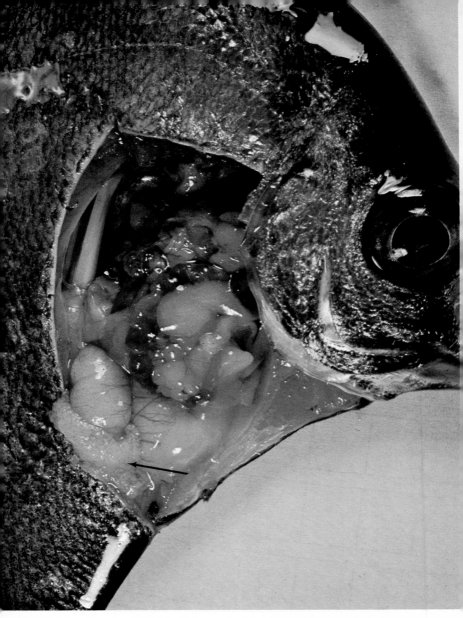

The location of the various abdominal organs will vary depending on the body shape of the particular fish. This specimen (*Monodactylus sebae*) had ripening eggs which can be seen emerging from one of the incised ovaries in the lower left hand corner (arrow) of the abdomen. Photo by Hiroshi Azuma.

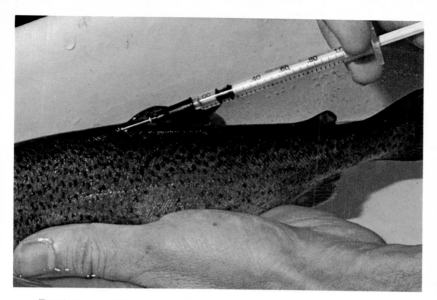

Freshwater fishes are often treated either by injection or by feeding them medicated food. Marine fishes lend themselves to treatment by immersion in an antibacterial solution because they drink water and hence the antibiotic in addition to absorbing the drug. Freshwater fishes on the other hand do not drink water. Photos by Doug Anderson.

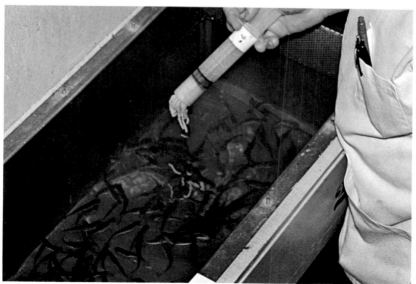

When the kidney becomes damaged, as occurs with a *Corynebacterium* infection, body fluids begin to accumulate. Exophthalmos (pop-eye) can be caused by the accumulation of excessive fluids behind the eye. Photo by Frickhinger.

festation of kidney damage, your internal examination might reveal a swollen kidney, and perhaps grossly visible lesions would be present. *Then* you can sit back and feel you are fairly close to diagnosis. Exophthalmos and ascites, plus obvious kidney damage—undoubtedly a bacterial infection which used the kidney as the target organ for reproduction. Kidney disease caused by *Corynebacterium* sp. would be a good tentative diagnosis. Now you have accomplished something.

If you want to freeze the kidney and have it submitted for confirmatory diagnosis based upon Gram's stain (small Gram-positive diplococci), cultural characteristics, or even histopathological examination, that is your perrogative. However, I would not encourage you to hold your breath while awaiting a definitive diagnosis. *Corynebacterium* species are very fastidious, require highly specific growth media, and generally take 7 to 10 days to grow on artificial media. If your other fishes are becoming listless and beginning to show signs of ascites and exophthalmos, get erythromycin and initiate treatment now—don't wait for the confirmatory laboratory diagnosis.

Now that you are convinced a thorough necropsy is a very important diagnostic procedure, let us continue with a brief description of the procedure in a step-by-step fashion.

EXTERNAL EXAMINATION

Skin: Examine the skin for external parasites or lesions such as raised scales, nodules, ulcers, nipping wounds, or reddened areas. A skin scraping should be done on the periphery of lesions, from beneath raised scales, behind fins, or any "suspicious" area on the fish. This material can be placed on a microscope slide along with a drop of *tank* water, coverslipped, and examined microscopically. Use tank water for this procedure, because tap water will cause a rapid change in hydrostatic pressure and cause unicellular parasites to "burst."

Fins: Careful examination of the fins is important, because many diseases cause a loss of tissue integrity. Frayed fins or reddening at the base of fins should be noted, as either is often a sign of a systemic bacterial infection. Frayed fins without reddening may indicate *Ichthyophonus* infection or attacks from more aggressive fishes.

The frayed caudal fin of this fish could have been caused by nipping from more aggressive fishes or by disease. A systemic bacterial infection often causes fraying and reddening of the fins. Photo by Dr. Herbert R. Axelrod.

By knowing the *normal* coloration of your fishes you can more readily determine when *abnormal* skin color develops. Photo by Hans and Klaus Paysan.

This fish shows abnormal mottling of the skin. Chronic bacterial diseases such as tuberculosis can cause abnormal skin coloration. Most fishes discolor upon death, shock or at night. Photo by Dr. Herbert R. Axelrod.

Body Openings: Carefully inspect the mouth for reddening or ulceration. A swollen or reddened vent area may indicate a gastrointestinal problem.

General Morphology: Fish are bilaterally symmetrical animals. If your dead fish is not bilaterally symmetrical, it is deformed. Deformations in body symmetry can be caused by a variety of conditions. A liver tumor, for example, can cause one side of a fish's abdomen to protrude farther than the opposite side. Don't just examine the fish from the side; look straight down at the fish to check for abnormalities. Exophthalmos (pop-eye) is more readily apparent when looking down at the fish.

Morphology can be altered in a symmetrical fashion as well. A swollen abdomen ("dropsy") can be caused by a variety of factors. Sometimes ascitic fluid causes the abdomen to swell. Liver malfunctions often cause a clear fluid accumulation, whereas peritonitis (an infectious process within the abdomen) will result in a foul-smelling creamy fluid accumulation. Enlargement of the air bladder can also result in abdominal swelling. Remember that not all

Not all cases of abdominal swelling are abnormal. The anemonefish in the lower portion of this photograph is gravid and has just begun to deposit her eggs on the side of the rock. Photo by Dr. Jens Meulengracht-Madsen.

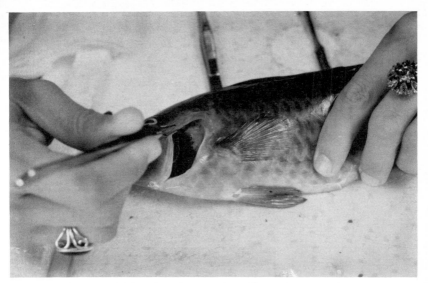

The gills should be closely examined for evidence of parasitism or anemia. Photo by Dr. Herbert R. Axelrod.

abdominal swellings are abnormal. If the fish recently engulfed a large quantity of food the abdomen may swell; females with developing ova also appear swollen. Don't throw a gravid female into the treatment tank and think the antibiotics should be responsible for reducing *her* abdominal swelling.

Gills: The gill should be red during life and shortly after death. Pale gills generally mean the fish is anemic. Look closely at the gill filaments. Parasites may be attached to the filaments and cause a ragged appearance. Secondary fungal infections are also often visible on the gills. If a microscope is available, remove a gill arch and then snip a small section of filaments from the arch. Place this on a microscopic slide with a drop of tank water and apply a coverslip. If small parasites are present, they can be most easily detected by using 100X and low illumination. If a microscope is not available, look at the gills with a magnifying lens.

Eyes: The eyes should be inspected for exophthalmos, lens or corneal opacities, and the presence of a white film.

Seahorses are also a marine fish and are subject to diseases just as other species of fishes. Photo by Hansen.

Congenital deformities of fish can be induced by a variety of adverse physical and chemical conditions as well as infectious diseases. These are all "Siamese" twins.

Poisonous invertebrates, such as this *Conus textile,* should not be placed in the marine aquarium because they are capable of killing fish and seriously wounding the aquarist who might unwittingly handle it. Photo by K. Gillett.

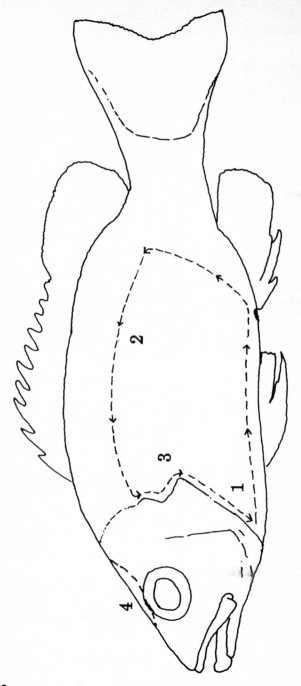

INCISIONS TO BE MADE IN DISSECTING A FISH

INTERNAL EXAMINATION

Once again I want to emphasize that before you can recognize the abnormal, you must be familiar with normal tissue appearance. Organ size, shape, and location may vary among various species, but once you have become familiar with the organ morphology, color, and texture in a particular species you should be able to look at a variety of fish types and know when obvious gross pathological changes exist. The illustrations in this book will help you locate the organs and get an idea of what is normal and abnormal, but you will have to dissect a few fishes yourself to gain any expertise in internal fish anatomy and pathology. If you are a successful fisherman, the usually arduous task of cleaning your catch can now be an exciting anatomy lesson. Perhaps you will even discover a disease situation and gain some experience in recognizing pathological changes as well. For example, approximately 80 % of fishes caught in the wild harbor at least one species of parasite. This may lead to a change of menu for your supper, but the knowledge you gain will make it worth the sacrifice.

You may prefer to modify the methodology and sequence of the internal necropsy procedure according to your preference and the instruments you are using. The step-by-step sequence which follows is the way I perform a fish necrospy. Whatever sequence you feel comfortable with will be best for you, if you remain consistent. If you fail to conduct the necropsy in a consistent, step-by-step fashion, you are likely to make mistakes or overlook a significant sign.

If you are working on the kitchen table, you might want to use some old newspapers. Hold the fish in dorsal recumbancy (on its back). Using a sharp scalpel or single-edged razor blade, make a very small incision just below the heart. Insert one blade of the scissors into this opening and lift up on the skin. Cut posteriorly along the ventral midline, lifting up with the buried scissor blade as you cut. This will reduce the chances of your puncturing the gastro-intestinal tract. When your incision reaches the vent area, cut upwards on the fish's left side. Continue this incision crani-

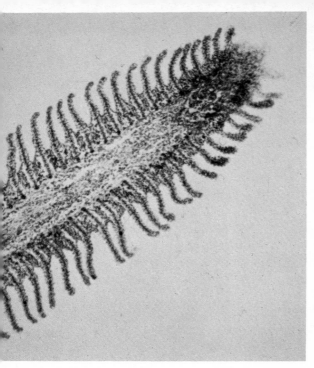

Left: A magnified stained histologic section of a normal gill filament.
Below: Histologic section showing damaged gills. Notice the total absence of gill lamellae at the base of the filament.

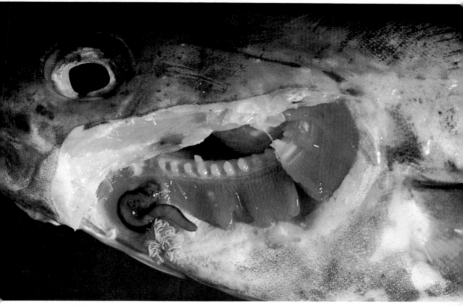

A parasitic copepod has attached itself to the gill region. These copepods have been known to burrow through the skin and penetrate the heart thereby causing the death of the host.

A magnified view of a portion of a gill arch reveals extensive damage to some of the gill filaments. When the gills are extensively damaged the normal respiratory functions are disrupted.

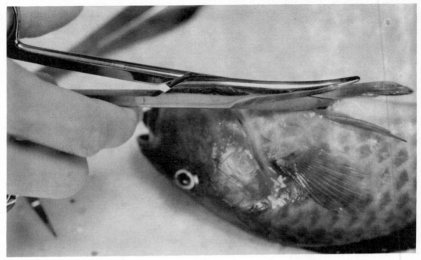

Lift up with the buried scissor blade as you cut so that you avoid puncturing the intestinal tract. Photo by Dr. Herbert R. Axelrod.

ally all the way to the gills so that you have essentially removed the left body wall of the fish.

Observe all visible body organs *in situ* before rearranging any of them with a probe. If you see any obvious abnormalities, record them now. Close-up photographers may want to wash their hands now and begin snapping that shutter. As with the external examination, let us proceed with the internal necropsy examination in a step-by-step fashion. I suggest you use the following sequence:

Peritoneal Cavity: Look at the abdominal wall and musculature for reddened areas or nodules. Check for fluid accumulation within the abdominal cavity (ascites).

Viscera Examination: Examine the entire gastro-intestinal (G.I.) tract from the esophagus to the anus. Make note as to whether there is food in the gut or whether the intestinal tract feels flaccid, fluid-filled; note the texture and coloration. Snip the esophagus and pull the G.I. tract posteriorly along with the attached liver, spleen, pancreas, and pyloric cecae. Cut the vent free of its muscular attachment and set all the viscera on a moist towel for later dissection.

Heart: Snip the heart free and look for lesions and areas of discoloration. Now is a good time to observe the blood of recent mortalities. The blood should be red, not chocolate brown. Brown blood indicates a methemoglobinemia, as occurs with nitrite toxicity.

Gonads: The gonads (sexual organs) are often hard to find, especially if the fish is not sexually mature. If you notice them lying across the air bladder, make note of the sex. The ovaries appear egg-filled, while the testes are white and exude milt if the male is "ripe." Abnormalities can occur in both the male and female reproductive tracts. Just as with birds, an "egg-bound" condition can occur in fishes which have a reproductive tract smaller than the eggs which they try to excrete.

Air (Swim) Bladder: Examine the air bladder, then remove it to expose the kidney.

Kidney: Check the kidney for obvious swelling, then remove the renal peritoneum (sheath encapsulating the kidney). Check for areas of necrosis and abscessation. Do not confuse the normal Corpuscles of Stannius with kidney lesions. Two corpuscles (compact oval structures) are *generally* present on the surface of most fishes' kidneys, although more than two can occur. Examine the ureters and urinary bladder for evidence of parasitism.

Liver and Gall Bladder: Now go back to the viscera you had previously removed and examine the liver and gall bladder for any pathological changes. If swelling or abscessation exists, record these findings. Cut into the liver and examine it internally as well. The gall bladder may be very swollen with greenish bile if the fish has not eaten recently. Parasites may be lodged in the bile duct, so examine thoroughly.

Spleen: Examine the spleen for enlargement, atrophy (reduction in size), and color change. In chronic diseases, the spleen is often dark and very enlarged with rounded edges, appearing somewhat like a football. Normally the spleen is elliptical, with sharp edges. In some diseases, abscesses may appear on or in the spleen.

All lesions should be considered as contagious unless you have shown that the disease is not infectious. Remove diseased fish from the exhibition tank and place them in the treatment tank until all clinical signs of disease are gone. Photo by Dr. Herbert R. Axelrod.

A heavy infestation of thorny-headed worms (acanthocephalans) can rapidly emaciate the host. The photo below is a magnified histologic section showing the proboscis of the worm imbedded in the host's intestine. When conducting a post-mortem examination, check for fibrotic nodules (lumps) in the intestinal wall. These nodules are often the site of worm attachment. Photo by Dr. J.C. Chubb.

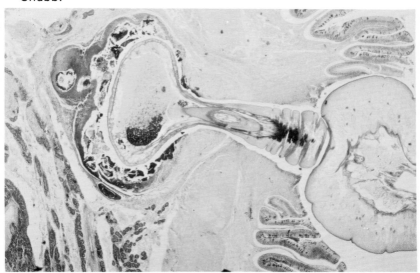

Remove the renal peritoneum and examine the kidney for evidence of disease. The kidney is located just below the pointer. Photo by Dr. Herbert R. Axelrod.

Internal G.I. Tract Exam: Run the intestine between your fingers and feel for nodules in the intestinal wall. Fibrotic nodules are often the site of thorny-headed worm attachment. Open the entire gut from the esophagus to the rectum and look for the presence of food, lesions, or parasites. If you find parasites you may want to preserve them for later identification. Generally 10% formalin is used for preservation, but rubbing alcohol or vodka also will work.

Brain: Using your scalpel or razor blade, cut off a portion of the cranium. If the cranium is hard, *don't* use the scalpel as a "pick," because a piece of the blade may break off and fly in your face (personal confession). Use forceps or tweezers to chip off the cranium of older, tougher fish. Look at the brain, checking for lesions and reddened areas. Systemic bacterial diseases can often invade the brain, leading to meningitis, or inflammation of the membranes surrounding the brain.

The Diagnosis and Treatment of Marine Fish Diseases

A definitive diagnosis is required before non-infectious diseases (such as high nitrite, low dissolved oxygen, or poor nutrition) can be accurately treated. It is not, however, always necessary to obtain a definitive diagnosis before *infectious diseases* can be properly treated.

The proper course of therapy can generally be selected from a tentative diagnosis based upon clinical signs and gross pathological changes. Ideally, it is best to isolate the causative organism, do drug sensitivity tests, and back the diagnosis with a myriad of clinical pathology tests and histopathological findings. This is not practical, however, especially if you only have one sick fish. It would be ludicrous to sacrifice the sick fish for a complete bacteriological and histopathological work-up so you could know what it had and how it should have been treated before you killed it. I am writing this book for *you*, the average saltwater aquarist. If you were an importer and hundreds of fish developed acute clinical signs of disease, I would encourage you to try for a definitive diagnosis. It would also be important in the latter case to do anti-bacterial sensitivity tests and try out the treatment on a few fishes prior to subjecting all of them to your drug of choice. The average saltwater aquarist, however, will generally need to rely on the powers of observation and rational thinking to diagnose fish disease conditions.

Every marine aquarist should have the capability to

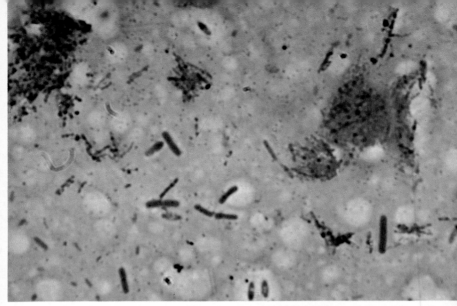

The acid-fast (red) bacteria are *Mycobacterium marinum* which were isolated from a fish which died of tuberculosis. Larger non-acid-fast bacteria are also apparent in this tissue imprint. Photo by Piscisan Ltd.

The very small Gram-positive (purple) diplobacilli were isolated from tissues of a fish with bacterial kidney disease.

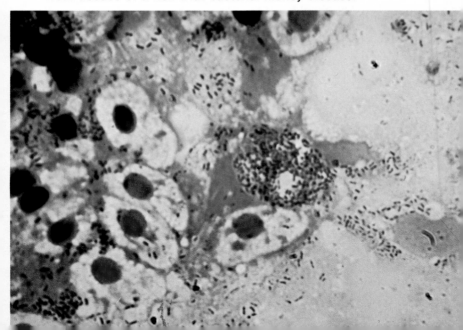

Saprolegnia is a fungus that invades dead tissues. This fish, *Scatophagus argus,* should be removed from the exhibition tank and treated both topically and systemically with anti-fungal agents. Photo by Frickhinger.

This microscopic wet mount preparation shows the *Saprolegnia* fungus to have numerous ramifying filaments. Photo by Dr. D. McDaniel.

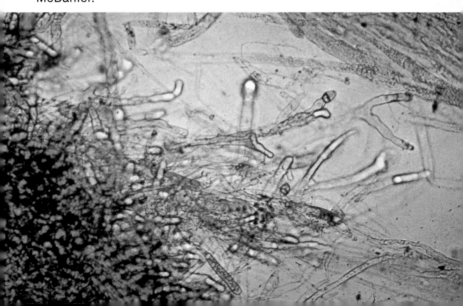

derive a tentative diagnosis from the clinical signs of disease in the living fish and from the gross pathological changes which occurred in the diseased fish. Remember, it is not necessary to diagnose a condition any further than is required to institute proper therapy. I strongly feel this approach is appropriate for the average saltwater aquarist. If you diagnose the disease to a bacterial infection, and treat with the appropriate antibacterial agent, that is all that counts. It is really of only academic interest for the individual aquarist to know whether it was an *Aeromonas* or a *Pseudomonas* infection.

As a practicing veterinarian specializing in aquatic animal medicine, my tendency is to rely heavily on clinical signs of disease. Unlike human medicine, where disease symptoms can be verbalized, veterinarians are forced to find out where lesions are without a conversation with the patient. In much the same way, you will need to rely heavily on the powers of observation to determine which disease you are confronted with and how it occurred.

I want this book to be as practical as possible, so I am not going to itemize the diseases in alphabetical order according to whether they are infectious (caused by an organism) or non-infectious (caused by an environmental condition). Furthermore, I will not categorically list the infectious diseases based upon whether they are caused by external, internal, or gill parasites or whether they are caused by bacteria, fungi, or viruses. Although this would be an orderly approach, I am afraid it would lead you to frustration and confusion.

You want to know the cause of the disease in order to select the proper course of therapy. The easiest way to establish the cause of disease is to observe the *clinical signs* and *pathological changes*. That is the order in which you will see them in your fish, so that is the way I am going to list them in this book. I am making no pretense that this is a comprehensive list of all the possible diseases which could occur in your aquarium; however, this list comprises the vast majority of the diseases which you are likely to encounter.

The fish's eyes should be closely examined for abnormalities. Defects in the iris of this fish could stem from a variety of infectious and non-infectious conditions including an inadequate diet. Photo by Dr. R.L. Sweeting.

Likewise, the treatments which I recommend are not a compendium of fish therapeutic agents. As research in aquatic animal medicine progresses, some of these drugs and treatment schedules will undoubtedly by replaced by more effective drugs designed specifically for treating exotic marine fishes. However, until those new drugs become available you will need to rely on the treatments which have been demonstrated to be effective by myself and other marine fish disease specialists.

Because of the tremendous species diversity and individual differences in drug susceptibilities, great care must be exercised in observing the effects of any treatment and good judgment used in stopping or modifying whatever seems inappropriate.

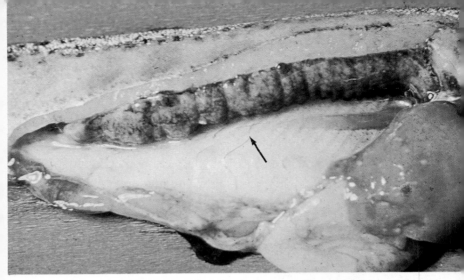

Notice the pale musculature and extremely swollen necrotic kidney (arrow) of this fish which died of an *Ichthyophonus* infection. Photo by Dr. P. Ghittino.

This photo shows the principal visceral organs of a diseased fish. The enlarged gall bladder (arrow) has blocked the view of the liver. An enlarged gall bladder generally means the fish has not eaten recently. The enlarged spleen (arrow, far right) is often seen in chronic infections.

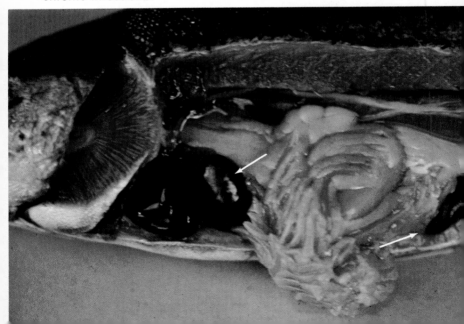

The cause of white spot disease of this fish was attributable to *Cryptocaryon irritans*. Whether the spots are caused by *Cryptocaryon* or *Oodinium*, copper sulfate therapy is the preferred treatment. Photo by Frickhinger.

Finquel® (tricaine methanesulfonate, Ayerst Laboratories) is a safe, effective fish anesthetic often used for euthanasia (painless death). Photo by Dr. Herbert R. Axelrod.

Fishes can be treated with drugs in a variety of ways. Most antibacterials can be given either orally, by injection, or by external application. It is quite stressful to capture a fish and give it antibiotics orally with an eyedropper. Medicated feed also has its drawbacks; sick fishes often will not eat any food, let alone an unpalatable drug/food combination.

Treating fishes by injection works well for large individuals, especially if they are anesthetized with 1:10,000, MS-222 (tricaine methanesulfonate, Sandoz Pharmaceuticals, Hanover, New Jersey) prior to handling. If an inexperienced aquarist tries to give injections to a small unanesthetized fish, problems are very likely to occur. This procedure would severely stress an already sick fish and probably cause the drug to be administered in the wrong spot.

Although some drugs must be given orally, most drugs I will be recommending are water-soluble and readily absorbed by the fish when placed in its aquatic environment. This method of treatment by absorption results in more consistent therapeutic levels of the selected drug, and should an adverse drug reaction occur, the fish can be removed promptly from the treatment solution.

Giving drugs by injection is not recommended for the beginning salt water aquarist. Photo by Dr. Herbert R. Axelrod.

All treatments, except copper therapy for white spot disease, are to be done in the quarantine/treatment tank and *not* in the exhibition tank. This treatment tank should be constantly ready for newcomers or for emergency conditions. The artificial sea water in the treatment tank must be kept aerated and have the same pH, salinity, and temperature as the main tank. In all but a few emergency situations, I recommend that you withhold food from the fish for 24 hours prior to handling, transfer, and treatment. I don't want to go into a big discussion on digestive physiology, but I do want to explain my justification for this recommenda-

Mucus covered fecal casts indicate that an intestinal problem exists. When a fish loses its intestinal mucous coat, bacteria can more easily invade the fish's body. Photo by Dr. Gerald R. Allen.

tion so you won't have guilt feelings about depriving the fish of its food.

The reason for a 24-hour fast prior to handling is to free the G.I. tract of food and feces. Capture, tank transfer, and adjustment to a new environment cause stress. The steroids (adrenalin) released into the bloodstream during stress cause a "fight-or-flight" reaction. Initially this reaction causes the gut to shut down in much the way your stomach gets a tight feeling during periods of anxiety. If the gut is filled with food, gut hypermotility often follows this stage, thereby causing diarrhea. Diarrhea and subsequent sloughage of the protective mucous lining of the gut results in the formation of mucus covered "fecal casts" which can sometimes be seen clinging to the fish's anus. Losing this protective mucous coat renders the fish more susceptible to bacteral invasion through the gut wall. Therefore, you should withhold food from fishes prior to treatment.

Many of the drugs recommended in this book can be obtained either directly from your local veterinarian or by prescription. Don't be surprised, however, if all you get is a blank stare when you ask your veterinarian for a 1:19,000 solution of malachite green. Chemicals whose medicinal use is generally limited to treating fish diseases, such as malachite green, can be more readily obtained from a tropical fish store. Fish stores are also more likely to have these medicinal agents in small packages designed for purchase by the aquarist. If you need to obtain the drugs from a pharmacy, be sure to explain the intended use to the pharmacist. In many instances the pharmacist will provide you with information on proper handling and storage of the drug so you can obtain maximum shelf life.

When medicating fishes, be sure the drug is properly mixed before pouring it into the treatment tank. This can best be accomplished by stirring the drug into a glass of water isolated from the tank. Pour this mixture across the surface of the water, stirring the tank water as your pour.

A relatively safe medication to be put in the exhibition tank is copper sulfate. Drugs should be dissolved in a glass of water before pouring them into the tank. Photo by Dr. Herbert R. Axelrod.

GASPING SYNDROME

Clinical Signs: Most of the fishes in the tank develop acute signs of distress, begin to jump or swim irregularly or become listless, gasp for air, and have rapid breathing with the opercles flared and the gills exposed.

Diagnosis: Nonspecific, could be hypoxia caused by inadequate level of dissolved oxygen stemming from such things as overcrowding, inadequate aeration, or elevated water temperature. These clinical signs of disease could also be the result of a poisoning, such as nitrite toxicity.

Treatment: Change the water immediately or remove fishes to any other suitable marine water. If you don't have your quarantine/treatment tank filled with suitable water (it should be constantly ready!), increase the aeration in the affected tank immediately. If the pump is not working, add a few drops of hydrogen peroxide or (if you're a scuba diver) use some compressed air while a new pump is being obtained.

Refillable, portable air tanks are commercially available for a back-up system in case of pump or power failure. Photo courtesy of Romeek Devices, Ltd., Portsmouth, Virginia.

Fish which have died of anoxia (suffocation or asphyxiation) have the mouth agape and the opercles flared. Photo by Dr. Herbert R. Axelrod.

Check the dissolved oxygen (D.O.) level; if the D.O. is adequate, check other water quality parameters. If water chemistry factors are within the acceptable limits, you should suspect a toxicity, re-evaluate your aquarium management, and begin making a complete change of water in the exhibition tank.

ANOXIA

Pathological Changes: Dead fishes have mouth agape, opercles flared, and pale gills; rigor mortis (body stiffening after death) sets in rapidly.

Diagnosis: Anoxia. In this situation the oxygen in the body tissues has been reduced to the point at which the fish can no longer survive.

Treatment: Increase the dissolved oxygen level; look for causes such as overcrowding, faulty pump, or decaying organic matter. If the tank water is cloudy, figure out what caused the bacterial or algal bloom. Correct whatever caused the decreased dissolved oxygen level.

NITRITE TOXICITY

Clinical Signs and Pathological Changes: Most of the fishes in the tank show evidence of anoxia. They are listless and breathe rapidly. Petechial hemorrhages (small red spots) develop on various tissues, particularly on the thymus (the thymus is located within the opercle, just above the gills). Post-mortem examination reveals chocolate brown blood.

Diagnosis: Methemoglobinemia from nitrite toxicity. Confirm this diagnosis by checking the ammonia nitrogen level in the tank. If the ammonia nitrogen or the nitrite level is higher than normal and you have not recently fed or stressed the fishes, a confirmatory diagnosis is secure. Feeding or stressing fishes results in increased excretion of nitrogenous wastes, and most of these wastes are eliminated by the gills in the form of ammonia. If the fishes' habitat is working properly, this momentary rise in ammonia nitrogen will subside once the beneficial bacteria in the biofilter have a chance to break it down to harmless elements.

The ammonia nitrogen level should be monitored with a test kit prior to feeding. Feeding often results in the increased release of metabolic wastes thus causing a temporary rise in ammonia nitrogen. Photo by Dr. Herbert R. Axelrod.

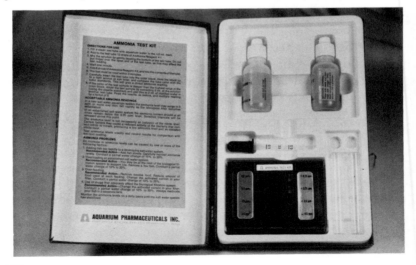

Treatment: Put acutely affected fishes in the treatment tank and add 1 ppm of methylene blue. This low dosage of methylene blue hastens the conversion of methemoglobin back to hemoglobin. The activity of methylene blue can be enhanced by the simultaneous use of ascorbic acid (Vitamin C). Add 250 mg of ascorbic acid to each 10 gallons of salt water in the treatment tank. Ascorbic Acid Injection, U.S.P., a sterile neutral solution of the vitamin, designed for parenteral (intravenous) injection, should be used; 5-ml ampules of this solution can be purchased from most veterinarians. Although the solution may lower the pH, leave the fishes in this solution until clinical signs of cyanosis stop.

Figure out what caused the toxic level of nitrite to accumulate in the exhibition tank. Since you never use antibiotics in this tank, the cause should not stem from the death of the beneficial bacteria (*Nitrobacter* sp. and *Nitrosomonas* sp.). If the tank is new, perhaps you either failed to seed the gravel with these organism or did not allow them the necessary two weeks to become established. Perhaps you recently added more fishes or invertebrates and thereby overcrowded the tank? If you exceeded the tank's carrying capacity, reduce the number of specimens. Changing the tank water is the best first aid for many aquarium problems, providing the new water is suitable.

ECTOPARASITISM
Clinical Signs: The fish may show rapid breathing and occasionally scratch the operculum. Gross examination reveals external parasites attached to the skin.

Diagnosis: Ectoparasitism caused by monogenetic flukes.

Treatment: If only a few parasites are present, try to remove them with tweezers. If a fish is heavily parasitized, the first treatment you should try is a freshwater bath. Prepare a freshwater bath by using aerated, chlorine-free tap water with the same temperature and pH as the aquarium. Tap water is generally less alkaline than sea water, so sodium bicarbonate (baking soda) may be needed to raise the pH. Leave the fish in the bath until the parasites fall off or until 3 minutes (maximum) have elapsed, unless the fish goes into shock before that time.

If the freshwater bath is not successful, prepare a formalin bath. Formalin is composed of 37% formaldehyde gas in a water/methanol solution. Add 1 ml (about 20 drops) of fresh formalin to each gallon of salt water in the treatment tank (1:3,800 concentration). If white sediment (paraformaldehyde) is in the bottle, this solution should not be used. Paraformaldehyde is toxic to fishes; its formation is accelerated by light and low temperature, so store formalin in a dark warm place.

Aerate this mixture vigorously for 24 hours prior to the bath; this provides a suitable dissolved oxygen level and will allow most of the methanol to go out of solution. Withhold food from the fish for this 24-hour period while the formalin bath solution is being aerated. Put the fish in the bath until the parasites are killed or until 30 minutes (maximum) have elapsed.

Crustaceans and worms are among the most common external parasites of marine fishes, but cases of parasitism of one fish by another also exist. Lampreys are one such marine parasite, but lamprey parasitism would be extremely unlikely in the marine aquarium. Photo by Dr. Mark P. Dulin.

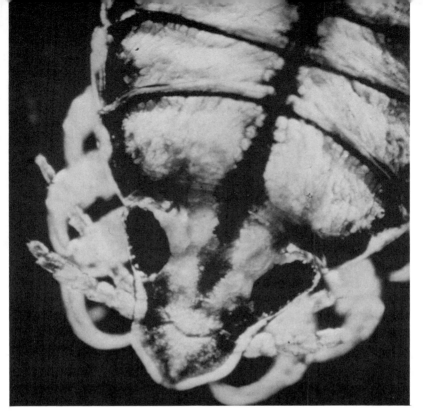

Parasitic isopods can infect fish in the ocean but are not likely to be a problem for the aquarist. These parasites are so large that they are grossly visible and could be removed with tweezers. Photo by Frickhinger.

COPEPOD PARASITISM

Clinical Signs: Copepods, or the egg sacs of copepods, are seen attached to either the gill filaments or the external surface of the fish. Cysts or sore spots may be evident where the parasite was anchored to the host. Some copepods cause severe skin erosion and have been known to penetrate through the skin and into the fish's heart. In these cases severe anemia and emaciation would also occur.

Diagnosis: Copepod parasitism. There are hundreds of species of parasitic marine copepods capable of burrowing into the flesh of fishes. These species have a variety of life cycles

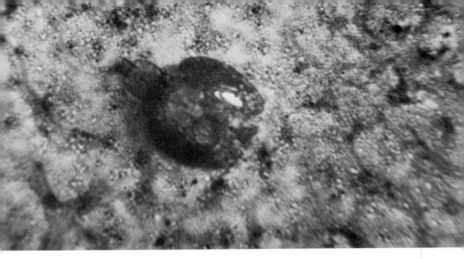

Copepod parasites are often not easily detected and can easily be introduced into the marine aquarium, especially if the aquarist fails to put new arrivals into the quarantine tank for a period of close observation. Photo by Dr. R. Pulin and C. Bridge.

and morphological characteristics. Dr. Z. Kabata has written an excellent book on parasitic crustaceans which describes the morphology and life cycles of many of these parasitic marine copepods (*Crustacea as Enemies of Fishes*, Book I in the Diseases of Fishes series, T.F.H. Publications).

Treatment: Although very common in the ocean itself, parasitism by marine copepods is uncommon in the carefully managed aquarium. There are a variety of contact insecticides which have been used to kill parasitic copepods. One successful course of therapy is a series of 2-day treatments with 1 ppm Dipterex (Dylox® or Chlorophos®). This treatment can be repeated once weekly for up to 3 more weeks, being sure to discard the treatment solution after each use. During the intervening 5-day period all fishes should be kept out of the exhibition tank so a "die-off" of the free swimming stages can occur. All the life stages of most parasitic marine copepod species are unable to survive a 20- to 30-day deprivation from a suitable host. This Dylox® therapy will kill the copepods, but the "head" of the parasite often remains embedded, thereby leaving an unsightly scar.

FUNGUS INFECTION

Clinical Signs: Fish has white to grey cotton wool-like lesions.

Diagnosis: Fungus infection (*Saprolegnia*).

Treatment: Fungus is generally considered to be a secondary invader; that is, areas of the fins or skin were injured or diseased before the fungus began to grow. Because fungus spores are generally ubiquitous (capable of appearing everywhere), the objective should be to kill the fungus on the lesion and restore the integument to a state of health. *Saprolegnia* is a saprophytic fungus capable of consuming an entire dead fish. It does not grow on healthy tissue but rather invades dead or dying tissues.

In addition to clearing up this infection, preventing its recurrence should be your prime objective. Evaluate the fish's dietary intake—is it getting enough vitamins, particularly vitamin A? Consider how the fin or skin became damaged and predisposed to fungal invasion—are other fishes "picking" on this one, or did the fish lose some of its protective mucus coat from rough handling or abrasions on coral?

To clear up the immediate problem of an invasive fungus infection, use a combination of swabbing the lesion with an antifungal agent and treating the fish with Furanace® . Agents used to *swab* the affected areas include:

1) Hydrogen peroxide
2) 2% Mercurochrome
3) Iodine solution (dilute 1 part commercial iodine tincture with 9 parts water)
4) Malachite green solution (1:15,000 concentration).

Affected fishes should also receive Furanace® therapy. By treating the fish with Furanace® in the water, the lesion is being attacked internally as well as externally, because Furanace® is readily absorbed into a fish's circulatory system. Furanace® is marketed for aquarium use by Abbott Laboratories, North Chicago, Illinois and is readily available at pet shops. The recommended dosage is 1 capsule of regular strength (3.8 mg) per 10 gallons of tank water. This drug will gradually deteriorate over the next 3 days. The treatment can be repeated every third day for up to a total of 3 treatments. Generally 6 days of treatment is sufficient.

WHITE SPOT DISEASE

Clinical Signs: In advanced stages of the disease, all or most of the fishes show signs of difficult respiration. Fishes may exhibit scraping movements, "flashing," or they may remain quiescent near the top of the tank and breathe rapidly. The skin and fins may develop small powdery or velvety dots which are best seen by refracted light in the early stages of the disease. If allowed to persist, larger ulcerated areas may form. The gills of mortalities may have visible white areas of infection. A wet mount of the gills may reveal large round to oval cells attached to the lamellae. Be sure and use a drop of tank water for the gill wet-mount preparation, as fresh water may rupture these cells. Examine the gill mount microscopically under low illumination.

Saprolegnia invades dead tissue that has been previously injured or diseased. Treatment of an affected fish such as the *Toxotes* shown here involves swabbing the affected area with an antifungal agent and a 5- to 6-day treatment with Furanace®.

When white spots begin to appear on the fins and skin the disease is in the advanced stages. Copper sulfate therapy is the only drug which should be put in the exhibition tank and then only after all invertebrates have been removed. Photo by Dr. John R. Randall.

Diagnosis: White spot disease caused by either *Oodinium ocellatum* (a parasitic dinoflagellate) or *Cryptocaryon irritans* (a ciliated protozoan).

Treatment: The treatment for white spot disease is 2 weeks of copper therapy. Because free-swimming infective stages of the causative organisms will be present in the exhibition tank, this disease is the one exception in which treatment of the fishes must be done in the display tank.

Copper sulfate is very toxic to invertebrates, so remove invertebrates prior to adding the copper. The invertebrates should be given a 1-minute freshwater bath prior to putting them into the quarantine/treatment tank. The invertebrates are not suitable for white spot disease organisms, but they may harbor the free-swimming stages. The freshwater bath will cause an abrupt change in hydrostatic pressure which will rupture the cells of these free-swimming stages.

Keep the biological filtration unit in operation, but remove and disinfect the activated charcoal filter, coral, and shells because these "tie-up" the free copper ions. The dolomite and gravel in the aquarium will also bind with copper, but because they harbor infective stages of the organism they should remain in the tank.

The actual therapeutic level of free copper ions should be 0.15 ppm plus/minus 0.03 ppm. Because of variabilities in factors affecting the binding of copper ions with other ions in the tank (water hardness, amounts of gravel, etc.), the *actual* copper ion level will differ from the *calculated* copper ion level. It is therefore essential to monitor the free copper ion concentration daily. The initial treatment will likely become rapidly bound. Check the copper ion concentration daily throughout this 2-week period. At no time should the copper level exceed 0.2 ppm.

Several companies have moderately priced colorimetric copper test kits available for saltwater aquarium use. For better accuracy, you should use a kit with a standard color disc range of 0 to 1 ppm. Hach Chemical Company has a modified Cuprethol test kit for determining copper levels in this range.

The mechanism by which copper rids the fish of external protozoans and dinoflagellates is via its irritating properties. Exposure to therapeutic levels of free copper ions causes copious amounts of mucus production on the skin and gill lamellae. The excessive mucus production entraps the organisms and, with the subsequent sloughage of the mucus (and organisms), these parasites are then exposed to the toxic effect of the free copper ions.

Excessive mucus production on the gills also interferes with respiration, so reduce the feeding level in order to decrease the fishes' oxygen demand. Make sure the tank is kept free of debris and has an adequate dissolved oxygen level.

After 2 weeks of copper therapy put the charcoal, shells, and coral back into the exhibition tank. Monitor the copper level, making sure the free copper ions are no longer present before replacing the invertebrates.

IMPAIRED CENTRAL NERVOUS SYSTEM

Clinical Signs: Chronic (slow) progression of clinical signs of disease, generally occurring in a solitary fish and not in the entire tank community. The fish gradually becomes more listless and exhibits signs of an impaired central nervous system. Jerking, twitching, and whirling dizzily about the tank are not uncommon signs. Many other non-specific clinical signs of disease appear in conjunction with this, such as frayed fins, exophthalmos, ulcerated skin, tucked-in abdomen (from emaciation), and poor coloration.

Diagnosis: Ichthyophonus infection. This disease is caused by an internal fungus; *don't* confuse this with *Ichthyophthirius* infection, the "ich" of freshwater fishes, which is caused by a ciliated protozoan.

Ichthyophonus infection is a systemic granulomatous infection of both marine and freshwater fishes and is caused

Fish infected with *Ichthyophonus hoferi* slowly develop clinical signs of an impaired central nervous system. Fish demonstrating bizarre behavior should be removed promptly from the exhibition tank.

by *Ichthyophonus hoferi*. The infectious process of this organism is not completely understood, but it appears to have the following life cycle: spores are ingested by the fish, whereupon they germinate and invade the gut lining. After penetration, these new hyphal bodies enter the blood stream for systemic distribution and spore production in new organs. Spores reach a new host after release to the external environment by ulceration or death and decay of the original host.

Treatment: A proved satisfactory cure for this condition has not yet been found. Under laboratory conditions, the spores of this organism have reportedly survived in salt water for 6 months and remained viable and infectious. By the time enough clinical signs have developed to diagnose ichthyophonus infection, the chances of a cure are minimal. If you are particularly fond of an infected fish and you don't think it is suffering, you might want to experiment with one of the antifungal drugs used in human and veterinary medicine. Amphotericin B (Fungizone®) has cured mammalian and some avian systemic fungal infections, so it might be worth a try. Controlled experiments have not yet been completed to test the efficacy of Fungizone® in fish.

Either treat or destroy this fish; do not allow it to remain in the exhibition tank. Healthy fishes often start to "pick" on sick fishes, and even the smallest skin lesion may be teeming with infectious stages of this parasite.

KIDNEY DISEASE

Clinical Signs and Pathological Changes: One or several fishes slowly develop ascites (abdominal swelling from fluid accumulation in the abdominal cavity) and have roughened scales. Unilateral or bilateral exophthalmos (pop-eye) may also occur. A post-mortem examination reveals ascitic fluid with possible necrosis and abscessation of the kidney. Abscesses may also occur on the liver and spleen.

Diagnosis: Kidney disease caused by *Corynebacterium* species.

Erythromycin is the preferred antibiotic for treatment of bacterial kidney disease. Erythromycin capsules have been prepared for aquarium use and can be purchased at pet stores.

Injectable Erythrocin® has the advantage of going into solution faster than the capsules, however Erythrocin® is not approved for use in fish; injectables can be obtained only by prescription. Photo courtesy of Abbott Laboratories.

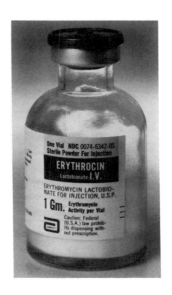

Treatment: This bacterial disease (and one other) is listed separately from other bacterial infections because the preferred treatment differs. *Corynebacterium* sp. is the only Gram-positive organism thus far found capable of causing epizootics in a marine aquarium. (The Gram stain is used to divide bacteria into 2 groups. Those bacteria which retain the crystal violet (appear purple) are said to be Gram-positive. Those bacteria which are decolorized by alcohol and take up the safranin counterstain (appear red) are said to be Gram-negative.) The other bacterial pathogens of fishes are all Gram-negative. In human and veterinary medicine, a drug is selected for use based upon its effectiveness against either the Gram negatives, Gram positives, or both. If the drug is effective against a wide variety of Gram negatives and Gram positives, it is considered to be a "broad-spectrum" antibiotic. In the case of kidney disease (and tuberculosis) there are drugs available which work better than these broad-spectrum antibiotics.

Because a tentative diagnosis can be made based upon the clinical signs and pathological changes of kidney disease, the preferred antibiotic (erythromycin) should be used. The dosage of erythromycin ethylsuccinate (Erythrocin®) is 250 mg per 5 gallons of tank water. Siphon 25 % of the water from the treatment tank every other day, refill with suitable salt water, then add an additional 200 mg of Erythrocin® per 5 gallons of tank water. This process should be repeated every other day for 5 to 7 days.

WASTING DISEASE

Clinical Signs and Pathological Changes: One or a few fishes slowly develop a "wasting" disease. They become listless, stop eating, and develop a "tucked-in" abdomen. Unilateral or bilateral exophthalmos may occur. The fishes develop frayed fins, raised scales, and blotchy areas of skin discoloration. Small skin lesions progress to large ulcerated areas. In the terminal stages of the disease, an infected fish retires to dark or secluded areas of the tank. Post-mortem examination generally reveals granulomatous lesions throughout the body organs. Bacteriological methods reveal the presence of acid-fast bacilli. Acid-fast bacilli are rod-shaped bacteria which do not decolorize upon the addition of acid alcohol. The acid-fast bacteria comprise the bacteria known as *Mycobacterium*.

Diagnosis: Tuberculosis caused by *Mycobacterium marinum*. Confirmatory diagnosis can be made by submitting tissues to a university diagnostic bacteriology laboratory or a private (and in some cases, hospital) laboratory. This is another bacterium which requires highly complex growth requirements and takes a long time to grow. You cannot afford to wait for confirmatory diagnosis to initiate treatment based upon your tentative diagnosis.

Treatment: Just as was the case for kidney disease, this bacterial disease is treated separately from other bacterial diseases because the treatment is specific. Broad-spectrum antibiotics do not produce satisfactory control of tuberculosis. The same drugs used in treating human tuberculosis (caused by *Mycobacterium tuberculosis, M. avium*, or *M. bovis*) are effective in controlling piscine tuberculosis caused by *Mycobacterium marinum*. Although *Mycobacterium marinum* has been isolated on occasion from human skin lesions, it is not considered to be a serious pathogen of man. Unlike tuberculosis of birds, cattle, or primates, this disease can be treated without risking human infection. The drugs of choice are those currently being used by many physicians to cure human tuberculosis. Prolonged therapy with isoniazid is recommended. Isoniazid is water-soluble and can be added to the treatment tank at the rate of 250 mg/5 gallons of salt water. Every third day siphon 25% of the water from the treatment tank, refill with suitable salt water, and add an additional 200 mg of isoniazid per 5 gallons of tank water. This course of therapy may need to be continued for 30 to 60 days.

Many humans are treated for tuberculosis with only isoniazid therapy. In many cases, however, the attending physician prescribes rifampin (Rifadin® , Dow Chemical or Rimactane® , Ciba Pharmaceuticals) in conjunction with isoniazid. Isoniazid plus rifampin generally brings about a

Fish suffering from tuberculosis develop a slow wasting condition as evidenced by a sunken abdomen. This saltwater catfish also has clouded eyes which may also occur in bacterial infections. Photo by Dr. Herbert R. Axelrod.

quicker cure in fishes than just using isoniazid. Unfortunately rifampin is not water-soluble and must be given orally. In addition, rifampin is expensive (about $1.00 per 300 mg. capsule). If your pharmacist will sell a single rifampin capsule (which is all you will need), cost is not the limiting factor, but generally a pharmacy has to special-order the drug and the smallest bottle contains 30 capsules.

Whether you decide to treat with isoniazid alone for 30 to 60 days or give rifampin-medicated food with the isoniazid will depend upon your individual circumstances. I have listed the procedure for preparing a fish food (Gordon's formula) which satisfactorily absorbs the rifampin and is palatable to most fishes.

1) Purchase 1 pound of fresh beef liver, a box of baby Pablum and a 300 mg. rifampin capsule. You will also need a blender, a 2-oz. measuring cup and some small containers for storing the medicated mixture.

2) Skin the liver of its fibrous covering and remove all tough connective tissue and blood vessels. Section the liver into half-inch cubes.

3) Put 2 ounces of cubed liver and 2 ounces of cold water into a blender and liquidize.

4) Pour the liquidized liver through a strainer and into a large bowl. Repeat this procedure until you have 10 ounces of this strained liver mixture.

5) Add Pablum to this mixture, stirring constantly until the mixture has the consistency of peanut butter.

6) Put the mixture into heat resistant containers and place the containers in a pan of water. Heat the water until it begins to boil; then turn off the heat and allow the containers to stand in the hot water for half an hour.

7) Pour the mixture from the containers into a large bowl. Add 50 mg. (one-sixth of the capsule) rifampin to this mixture and stir well.

8) Put this medicated food into small jars, label the jars "Rifampin-medicated food," and refrigerate.

9) Feed this mixture to the diseased fishes every other day for the duration of the isoniazid therapy.

One of the most obvious clinical signs of an acute systemic bacterial infection is frayed fins with reddening at the base of the fin. Severely eroded fins will regenerate once the infectious process has ended.

BACTERIAL DISEASE

Clinical Signs and Pathological Changes: Fishes have frayed or eroded fins and reddened areas on the base of the fins. The vent may be inflamed and swollen and long fecal casts of mucus may cling to the fish's anus. Reddening may also be seen along the lateral line or around the mouth. The eyes may be clouded and exophthalmos may occur in later stages. An epizootic may occur in which most of the fishes develop signs of disease. Pathological changes which may be seen are reddened areas on many of the body tissues, including the brain. The liver and spleen are generally enlarged, as evidenced by rounded edges of the organ rather than the normal sharp edge.

Diagnosis: Acute systemic bacterial infection.

Treatment: Remove all affected fishes and place them in the treatment tank. If the majority of the fishes are ill, you may need to resort to a rather drastic treatment and sterilization procedure. If the causative bacterium is also an ·aquatic saprophyte, the water may appear cloudy from its rapid multiplication. This may be a case in which poor aquarium management allowed the tank to become a center for disease amplification. In this instance a sterilization unit, such as an effective ultraviolet light sterilizer, would be of value. If you have no sterilization unit or are in doubt as to its effectiveness, you may want to resort to complete sterilization of the exhibition tank with a chemical agent such as Wescodyne® or Clorox®.

Tank sterilization is a serious and troublesome event which will upset your former biological balance. Check your management procedures to figure out how this pathogen was introduced. If you feel a drastic approach is warranted, then proceed in the following manner:

1) Place all live specimens in the treatment tank and begin therapy with a broad-spectrum antibiotic such as Chloromycetin® , gentamicin, kanamycin, or neomycin.

2) Siphon the tank and place all plastic decorative items aside for washing and disinfection.

3) Fill the tank with tap water and add a disinfecting agent. Ordinary household Clorox® will suffice at ½ ounce per gallon of water. Let this solution circulate for 24 hours.

4) Neutralize the chlorine with granular sodium thiosulfate. This is available as "hypo" at photography stores. Add 1 ounce of this "hypo" to each 20 gallons of water and allow a 4 hour circulation time.

5) Siphon out this solution.

6) Rinse the tank and gravel with several changes of tap water.

7) Refill the tank with tap water for a final circulating 6-hour rinse.

8) Drain this water and add synthetic salt water.

9) Re-inoculate the gravel with the beneficial bacteria (*Nitrosomonas* sp. and *Nitrobacter* sp.) from a non-infected established gravel bed or biofilter. If no bacteria are available, use cultured bacteria tablets such as Envirotrol-F (Mardel Labs, Carol Stream, Illinois), or Nitro-Quik (Hawaiian Marine Imports, Houston, Texas).

Treat the diseased fishes and invertebrates with a broad-spectrum antibacterial agent. I recommend you avoid using Oxytetracycline (Terramycin®), the penicillin group, or the sulfa drugs. As I mentioned before, these antibiotics have had previous low-dosage use by aquarists, and many drug-resistant strains have now developed. Any one of the following four broad-spectrum antibiotics should provide beneficial results:

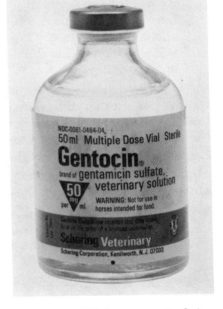

None of the four broad spectrum antibiotics I have recommended are approved by the Food and Drug Administration for use in edible or aquarium fish, even though your marine aquarium fishes are not likely to be used for human consumption. Gentocin® is one of the broad spectrum antibiotics which can be obtained from a veterinarian. Photo courtesy of Schering Corporation.

1) Chloramphenicol sodium succinate (Chloromycetin®) at the rate of 250 mg/5 gallons of salt water. Siphon 25 % of the water from the treatment tank every other day, refill with suitable salt water, then add an additional 200 mg of Chloromycetin® per 5 gallons of tank water. This process should be repeated every other day for 5 to 7 days.

2) Gentamicin sulfate (Garamycin®) at the rate of 250 mg/5 gallons of salt water. Siphon 25 % of the water from the treatment tank every other day, refill with suitable salt water, then add an additional 200 mg of Garamycin® per 5 gallons of tank water. This process should be repeated every other day for 5 to 7 days.

3) Kanamycin sulfate (Kantrex®) at the rate of 250 mg/5 gallons of salt water. Siphon 25% of the water from the treatment tank every other day, refill with suitable salt water, then add an additional 200 mg of Kantrex per 5 gallons of tank water. This process should be repeated every other day for 5 to 7 days.

4) Neomycin sulfate at the rate of 250 mg/gallon of salt water. Siphon 25% of the water from the treatment tank every other day, refill with suitable salt water, then add an additional 200 of neomycin per gallon of tank water. This process should be repeated every other day for 5 to 7 days.

If the causative agent is susceptible to the antibiotic, improvement should be noted within 3 to 5 days. The treatment should be continued for a minimum of 5 days otherwise the hardy bacteria may survive and the disease may recur. Overtreatment, on the other hand, can kill off the fish's normal flora and thus render it more susceptible to non-bacterial infections.

If the majority of fishes in the tank develop clinical signs of an acute bacterial infection, it would be advisable to remove all the fish and treat them with antibiotic therapy. In an extreme epizootic, complete disinfection of the exhibition tank may be warranted.

GAS-BUBBLE DISEASE

Clinical Signs and Pathological Changes: Most or all the fishes in a *cold*water marine aquarium develop minute to large bubbles within any of the external body surfaces including the fins, inside the mouth, and below the surface of the eye. Exophthalmos often occurs from air pressure behind the eye. Because of the subcutaneous air, moribund fishes are seen floating rather than sinking. When mortalities are held up to a light source, minute bubbles are seen, particularly within the fins.

Diagnosis: Gas-bubble disease caused by oxygen or nitrogen supersaturation. This diagnosis can be further substantiated if the pump or power filter on the *cold*water marine aquarium has developed a leak on the intake side. Check the level of dissolved oxygen; if it is supersaturated, chances are that the level of free nitrogen is supersaturated also.

Treatment: I have discussed gas-bubble disease with Dr. Herbert R. Axelrod, who has had long experience with all types of aquarium situations, and he has never seen a case of gas-bubble disease in any tropical aquarium. This disease would be an extremely unlikely possibility in a marine aquarium; the only reason I am including it in this book is because it has been overemphasized in the aquarium literature. Many aquarists are now paranoid about gas-bubble disease and are likely to jump to the conclusion that a fish with exophthalmos and bubbles adhering to the surface of the fish is suffering from gas-bubble disease. Gas bubbles adhering to the *surface* of a fish is not gas-bubble disease. If cooler water is added to the tank, bubbles will form as the solution warms and may adhere to the mucus layer of the fishes' skin. You can easily observe this phenomenon by filling a glass with cold tap water and allowing it to warm to room temperature. As the water warms, bubbles will appear and then leave the solution. That is because cold water holds more gas than warm water; remember that the warmer the tank water, the lower its oxygen-carrying capacity. It is very difficult to force enough gas into solution in a warmwater marine aquarium to produce clinical signs of gas-bubble disease, but the disease becomes a possibility in a *cold*water marine aquarium.

Gas-bubble disease is responsible for the death of millions of young trout and salmon each year. As the smolts migrate to the ocean, they are subjected to nitrogen supersaturation at the outfall of many hydroelectric dams. Many of these fishes are just momentarily stunned and could be revived with decompression treatment, but instead they become easy prey for sea gulls and carnivorous fishes.

Gas-bubble disease occurs in captive fishes generally because the power filter pump of a coldwater aquarium develops an air leak on the intake side. The air entering a loose connection or faulty seal can produce a supersaturated condition of both oxygen and nitrogen. This gas supersaturation produces a condition in fishes similar to the "bends" which scuba divers get when they surface too quickly without decompression stops. These tiny air bubbles enter the capillary beds and may coalesce to form large bubbles which can lodge in major vessels. When these air emboli block circulation to vital organs, death can occur.

The treatment procedure will vary depending on the severity of the clinical signs of gas-bubble disease. If the fishes are affected only to a minor degree, repair or removal of the faulty pump, plus vigorous agitation of the water, may be all that is required.

Although unusual, some aquarists have compression chambers which they use for bringing fishes up from the depths. If gas-bubble disease occurs, such a compression chamber would be useful to help force the gas emboli out of the fish's body. Photo by Dr. Herbert R. Axelrod.

INTESTINAL WORMS

Clinical Signs and Pathological Changes: Progressive emaciation ("wasting") with no other clinical manifestations of disease. Post-mortem examination reveals a large number of worms in the intestinal tract. Some species of worms may perforate the intestinal wall and cause peritonitis (an abdominal infection).

Diagnosis: Intestinal tapeworm or roundworm infection.

Treatment: Upwards of 80% of all wild fishes have some degree of parasitism, with many of these parasites residing in the gastro-intestinal tract. The successful parasite will not damage the host to the point of death, or else its "grocery store" will be gone. Some parasites, however, "commit suicide" by depleting the fish of nutrients to a point at which the fish dies. It is usually in these instances that the aquarist discovers parasites in the post-mortem examination. Roundworms and thorny-headed worms can be removed by treating the fish with piperazine-impregnated food at the rate of 25 mg/10 grams of food. Treatment should be given daily for a period of 10 days. Tapeworms (cestodes) can be effectively removed by treating the fish with Yomesan® (Chemagro Corp.) at the rate of 50 mg/10 grams of food. Withhold food 24 hours prior to treatment. A single dose of Yomesan® is generally effective in killing adult tapeworms. Although piperazine and Yomesan® are relatively non-toxic to fishes, the deworming treatment does involve a minimal risk. If a fish is heavily parasitized, a massive die-off of the parasites could result in an intestinal blockage and thus cause the death of their host.

LYMPHOCYSTIS

Clinical Signs: One to several fishes develop wart-like lesions on the body surfaces. Some lesions may resemble cauliflower, while others are separate white to gray firm nodules. The lesions are often seen on the fins and about the mouth.

Diagnosis: Lymphocystis, caused by a pox virus.

Fish with lymphocystis lesions should be quarantined until all lesions have healed. This disease is caused by a contagious pox virus and is untreatable, though a vaccine is a possible preventative treatment. Photo by Dr. J.E. Harris.

Treatment: Remove affected fishes, as lymphocystis is a contagious viral disease. Other fishes can presumably become infected by either ingesting the lymphocystis cells that flake off the fish or by absorbing the viral particles when these giant cells burst. The viral particles then invade certain cells situated beneath the skin. These cells hypertrophy (enlarge) as the virus takes over their normal machinery. Infected fishes should be quarantined for a minimum of 2 months while their immune response brings about a spontaneous cure. If lesions about the mouth become so severe as to interfere with eating, they can be surgically removed or treated with liquid nitrogen application in the same manner in which human and animal warts are removed. In either case the fishes should have no food for 24 hours and should be anesthetized with 1:10,000 MS-222 (tricaine methanesulfonate, Sandoz Pharmaceuticals, Hanover, New Jersey), prior to removal of the growth.

Quick-Reference Conversion Tables

Table of Household Measures

Measure	Approximate Metric Equivalent
1 drop	1/20 ml
1 teaspoon	5 ml
1 tablespoon	15 ml
1 pint	473 ml
1 quart	946 ml
1 gallon	3,785 ml

Parts Per Million Equivalents

ppm = 1 mg per liter water

ppm = 1 gram per 264 U.S. gallons.water

ppm = 0.0038 gram/U.S. gallon of water

ppm = 0.0038 ml/U.S. gallon of water

Using 1 % Stock:

ppm = 0.38 ml per U.S. gallon

ppm = 8 drops per U.S. gallon

1 % Solutions in Water

10 grams per liter

1 gram per 100 ml

0.1 gram per 10 ml

0.01 gram (10 mg) per 1 ml

Abbreviations

ml = milliliter

% = parts per hundred

pH = hydrogen ion concentration

ppm = parts per million

Recommended Reading

Amlacher's Textbook of Fish Diseases by Drs. D.A. Conroy and R.L. Herman. T.F.H. Publications.

Diseases of Fishes: Book 1: Crustacea as Enemies of Fishes, by Dr. Z. Kabata. T.F.H. Publications.

Diseases of Fishes: Book 2: Bacterial Diseases of Fishes by Drs. G.L. Bullock, D.A. Conroy, and S.F. Snieszko. T.F.H. Publications.

Diseases of Fishes: Book 4: Fish Immunology by D.P. Anderson. T.F.H. Publications.

Exotic Marine Fishes by Dr. Herbert R. Axelrod and C.W. Emmens. T.F.H. Publications.

The Marine Aquarium by Dr. Wolfgang Wickler. T.F.H. Publications.

The Marine Aquarium in Theory and Practice by Dr. C.W. Emmens. T.F.H. Publications.

Saltwater Aquarium Fish by Dr. Herbert R. Axelrod and W.E. Burgess.

Starting with Marine Invertebrates by Jerry G. Walls. T.F.H. Publications.

Poisonous Marine Animals by Dr. Findlay Russell. T.F.H. Publications.

INDEX

(Entries set in **bold** face denote illustrations.)

Immunization, 10
Injection, **71**, 96, **97**
Isoniazid® , 115

K

Kanamycin sulfate, 64, **67**, 120
Kidney, 85, **88**, **94**
Kidney disease, **63**, 72, **90**, 112, 113

L

Liver, 85
Lymphocystis, 123, **124**

M

Mechanical filtration, 18
Meningitis, **63**
Methemoglobinemia, 85, 102

N

Necropsy, 65, 81
Neomycin sulfate, 64, 120
Nitrite toxicity, 85, 102, 103

O

Oodinium, 31, **37**, **38**, 60, 109

P

pH, 18
pH test kit, **18**

Piperazine, **55**, 123
Poisonous invertebrates, **79**

Q

Quarantine, **32**, **34**, 37, 40, **44**, 53, 57, 60

R

Rifampin, 115, 116
Roundworms, **47**, **54**, 123

S

Skin, 73, **74**, **75**
Species compatibility, 19
Specific gravity, 20, 21, 23, 24
Spleen, 85, **94**
Swim (air) bladder, **47**, 76, 85

T

Tank capacity, 56
Tank disinfection, 57, 118
Tapeworms, **58**, **59**, 123
Thorny-headed worms, **55**, **87**
Tuberculosis, **90**, 114, **115**

W

White spot disease, **38**, **95**, 108, **109**

Y

Yomesan ® , **58**, 123